I0157144

The MacHamlet Trilogy

Three Comedies for Stage

The MacHamlet Trilogy

Three Comedies for Stage

MacHamlet

Bard Again!

MacHamlet Goes West

ഃ ഃ ഃ

John Owen Smith

The MacHamlet Trilogy
First published as separate playscripts
This combined edition published November 2015

Typeset and published by John Owen Smith
19 Kay Crescent, Headley Down, Hampshire GU35 8AH

Tel: 01428 712892
wordsmith@johnowensmith.co.uk
www.johnowensmith.co.uk

© John Owen Smith 2011–2015

*All rights reserved. No part of this publication may be reproduced by
any means, electronic or mechanical, including photocopy or any
information storage and retrieval system without permission in writing
from the publisher.*

***Permission from the above address should be sought before any
performance of these plays is contemplated.***

For further plays by the same author see www.johnowensmith.co.uk

ISBN 978-1-873855-72-0

Printed by CreateSpace

Introduction

I had already written twelve pantomime scripts, and was being asked for more. But to be fair, there are only so many variations on a traditional pantomime theme that one can write.

So a heinous thought occurred to me.

The ending to Shakespeare's *Hamlet* had always seemed to me to contain a certain element of pantomime ('He's behind you!') and the urge to build on this became irresistible, despite dire warnings from illustrious sources.

And what better combination than to mix it with the play that dare not speak its name?

In the *MacHamlet* series, the characters from the Bard's plays put aside their local differences for a while to face a common foe.

And the three Witches add a fourth dimension to the plots.

John Owen Smith
Headley Down
November 2015

The three plays which comprise the *MacHamlet* trilogy
were first performed by Headley Theatre Club
over the period 2011–2015

The cast ensnare the author before the start of a show

Contents

The Danish team prepare for action

MacHamlet

A rather unusual tale about a football match

Part 1 of the MacHamlet trilogy

MacHamlet

Cast List

The Scottish Team:

Mac Macbeth .... opportunist goal-seeker

Beth Macbeth .... his wife, team director

Witch One (Morag) .... organiser of Scottish cheerleaders

Witch Two (Kirsty) .... a cheery cheerleader

Witch Three (Bella) .... a dour cheerleader

Duncan King .... team captain

Banquo the Ghost .... a phantom winger

Birnam Wood .... from where we get defence

Glen & Morangie .... supporters of the Scottish distilleries

Will McGonagall [can double] .... a barred bard

The Danish Team:

Hamlet .... formerly known as Prince, dead ball specialist

Gertrude .... Hamlet's mother, now married to Claudius

Claudius .... disputed team captain

Horatio .... a solid goalkeeper

Yorick .... good with the head

Polonius .... trainer/manager

Ophelia .... team masseuse

Carl & Berg .... probably the best lager louts in the world

Hans Christian Andersen [can double] .... a seller of tales

Lady Godiva .... the referee from Coventry

Skye Blue .... a media correspondent

Plus cameo roles in Act I, Scenes 4 & 7 which can all be doubled

The year is 1040 and, strangely, so is the time!

List of Scenes

Act I

**** INTERVAL ****

Act II

The three witches run through the three plays

MacHamlet

Act I Scene 1 The Witches convene

(The three witches declaim from different points in the auditorium.)

Witch 1 Thrice the brindled cat hath mew'd.

Witch 2 Thrice and once the hedge-pig whined.

Witch 3 Harpier cries, "'Tis time, 'tis time."

Witch 1 'Tis time to start our pantomime!

Witch 2 Our pantomime of legends mixed.

Witch 3 Of vengeance vile and matches fixed.

(They begin to move towards the front of stage)

Witch 1 Of 2-3-5 …

Witch 2   … and 4-4-2

Witch 3 And chanting "Ee-aye-adio"!

Witch 1 We're bringing football to the Scots…

Witch 2 … because we like it lots and lots …

Witch 3 Even though you'll say, I bet …

All   It hasn't been invented yet!

Witch 1 Upon the heath a bothy lit.

Witch 2 A bothy blue, and out of it …

(We hear the whoosh of a Tardis landing)

Witch 3 … there came a man with powers that shocked, a man who called himself …

All   … the Doctor.

Witch 1 With him we whirled through time and space,

Witch 2 To light upon the strangest place.

Witch 3 A stadium where grown men play,

Witch 1 And now we're hooked – so you may say …

(All sing)   We're football crazy, we're football mad,
                That football game has taken awa'
                The little bit of sense we had –
                And it would take a dozen servants
                To wash our clothes and scrub,
                Since we became a member of
                That terrible football club.

Witch 1 Hubble, bubble, toil and trouble.

Witch 2 We are going to win the double.

Witch 3 With a team drawn from the lees
             Of William Shakespeare's tragedies.

Witch 1 By the pricking of my thumbs,
             Something wicked this way comes.
                   Open, locks,
                   Whoever knocks!

(Hamlet enters SR to 'Air on a G string' and slowly starts to light up a small cigar.)

Witch 2 Wicked! It worked. On with the show.

Witch 3 *(To audience)* See you later. Cheerio!

(The witches exit)

Act I Scene 2 **Hamlet meets Beth** *(Front of tabs)*

   (The stage manager enters quickly SR and takes the cigar from Hamlet.)

Stage Manager Sorry, no smoking. You ought to know that.

(The music stops)

Hamlet You mean because there is a law against it?

Stage Manager No, I mean because tobacco hasn't been discovered yet. It's 1040. Didn't they teach you any history at school? *(Exits)*

Hamlet No, because schools haven't been invented yet either. Only 1040 eh? *(Looks at his watch)* Bit early perhaps – but still *(takes out a can of Carlsberg and opens it)* who cares – never really too early is it?

(Enter SL Beth)

Beth Wha's tha' you're drinking?

14

Hamlet *Tha'* is probably the best lager in the world, madam.

Beth Lager? Call tha' a drink? Gnats could do better. *(She gets out a bottle of Scotch)* Now this is wha' I call a drink!

(She opens the bottle and wafts it under Hamlet's nose)

Smell the strength in tha'. None of your quick-brew here.

Hamlet There's nothing quick about brewing the way we do it in Elsinore.

Beth Twenty years old this is, laddie. Twenty. It's probably older than you are, and more mature.

Hamlet I would rather be blond with a bit of a fizz than stuck in a dour Scottish cellar for twenty years.

Beth There's the trouble wi' you continentals – impulsive – all mouth and trousers. Are you here for the festival?

Hamlet The festival of the Bard, yes.

Beth Yer no' that Romeo chap?

Hamlet Not at all! I am the eponymous Hamlet.

Beth Eponymous? Never heard of him.

Hamlet The great Dane.

Beth Ah, so ye'll be going to Crufts then?

Hamlet You are ignorant – what play do you come from?

Beth The play wi' no name.

Hamlet The play wi' no name? So I am eponymous and you are anonymous.

Beth Very good! Ye'll be a Bard yerself some day. I mean it's the play that no man dare name.

Hamlet But you are a woman.

Beth Aye. Oh well, I suppose it's all right then – I can tell you – it's Macbeth.

(Blackout and sounds of thunder)

Beth Woops. Perhaps not. It's only a silly superstition really you know. Can we have our lights back again please?

(Lights return)

Beth Thank you kindly. *(To Hamlet)* I'm Beth, wife of – that person whose name I just said. Now, d'you want to try the whisky or not?

Hamlet If you insist.

Beth If I insist? I offer you a dram of the finest single malt and all you can say is: "If you insist!" Philistine! But as I've just finished the bottle, we'll have to go to the pub for some more.

Hamlet Where is the pub?

Beth Conveniently situated behind these curtains.

Hamlet *(as they exit together SR)* Do you think they sell lager?

Beth I'll pretend I didn't hear tha'!

(They exit as curtains open)

Act I Scene 3 In a Scottish pub *(Full Set)*

The pub is populated with revellers

Macbeth Now since my wife's not here to stop me, I'll tell you a story.

Glen Aye, Mac, tell us a story.

Morangie Make it a good one.

Macbeth I was walking home across the moors, see, and I came upon these three weird women.

Morangie What way were they weird, Mac?

Macbeth What way? In a sort of witch way.

Glen Which way?

Macbeth Sort of.

Glen You've lost me.

Macbeth I wish.

Morangie Ignore him, Mac – he's ignorant.

Glen Well, if I'm ignorant what does that make you?

Macbeth D'you want to hear this story or no?

Glen Aye, Mac, we're listening.

Morangie There were three weird women, you said.

Macbeth That's right.

Glen On the moors.

Macbeth Aye, on the moors. And one said to me …

Morangie When's your wife coming?

Macbeth Are you telling this story, or am I?

Morangie Sorry boss – just didn't want you getting into trouble.

Glen You know what she's like if she catches you telling tales.

Morangie She'll murder you!

Glen Aye, murder most foul.

Macbeth If you don't let me finish this story, likely I'll murder <u>you</u>.

Morangie Sorry boss – carry on.

Macbeth So, this one comes up to me and says: "Are you up for a game of football?"

Glen Football? What's tha'?

Macbeth My words precisely. And the second one said: "It's the game of the future."

Morangie Wha' do we want with games? What's wrong with good old-fashioned rape and pillage?

Macbeth And the third one said: "In the future they won't let you rape and pillage so you'd better get used to football instead."

Glen No rape and pillage – where's the fun in that?

Morangie So what exactly is this football game then?

Macbeth The rules are very simple: if it moves, kick it – if it doesn't move, kick it until it does.

(Duncan moves forward)

Duncan Wha' are ye talking about, you wet, woolly, whippersnapper?

Glen It's football, Dunc.

Duncan *(Giving him a slap)* Who said you could call me Dunc. Only my friends call me Dunc. You can call me Mr King.

(Glen goes to retaliate, but Morangie pulls him back)

Morangie It's no' worth the sweat, Glen. Let him be. <u>Mr</u> King.

Macbeth *(To Duncan)* It's the future, Duncan. You kick your opponents to death instead of stabbing them.

Duncan Where's the pleasure in that?

Macbeth And instead of having to find hundreds of men, you only need to find eleven.

Glen Plus substitutes. I was listening.

Macbeth Plus substitutes.

Duncan You're mad! And who leads this army of eleven, plus substitutes?

Macbeth A captain.

Duncan A captain. So, you're demoting me to a captain, are you?

Macbeth Who says you'll be doing the leading?

Duncan Outside, and I'll show ye who'll be doing the leading!

(Banquo and Birnam come forward)

Banquo Any trouble, Boss?

Duncan Nothing I can't deal with. Mac here thinks he can take my place.

Birnam Getting cocky, are we, Mac?

Macbeth I've studied the opposition.

Duncan Oh, we have opposition lined up already do we? Who is it we have to kick to death?

Macbeth The Danes.

Banquo What, the ones who come in boats?

Birnam And rape and pillage?

Macbeth No more of that. We're challenging them to a game of football instead.

Duncan Who says?

(The Witches enter SL)

Witch 1 <u>We</u> say!

Witch 2 Any questions, ducky?

Witch 3 Or would you prefer a fillet of fenny snake stuck somewhere painful!

(They exit SR)

Macbeth <u>They</u> say.

Banquo Did I see what I thought I saw?

Birnam I saw three witch come sailing by.

Duncan I'm still the captain.

Macbeth You can be captain – Banquo's a winger and Birnam Wood ...

Birnam Aye?

Macbeth From Birnam Wood we get defence.

Duncan And you?

Macbeth Me, I'm an opportunist goal-seeker.

Duncan Right, but you'll get no goal-seeker's allowance, ye ken.

Banquo Where's the opposition?

(Beth and Hamlet enter SR)

Macbeth I think it's just arrived!

Beth *(To Hamlet)* Now I'll show you a real man's drink. *(To the bartender)* Two drams, and make them large ones.

Macbeth Who's your friend, Beth?

Beth He's a beer-swilling hun who I'm leading on the road to redemption.

Hamlet I am from Elsinore.

Duncan Elsinore? Where's tha'?

Hamlet Denmark.

Banquo He's a Dane – it <u>is</u> the opposition!

Birnam There's only one of him. Where's the rest?

Beth *(Giving a glass of whisky to Hamlet)* That'll put feathers on your chest. Sláinte!

Hamlet Skol!

(They both drain their glass in one – and Hamlet gasps for breath)

Macbeth *(To Hamlet)* That's not your usual tipple then.

Hamlet It is poison!

Duncan We don't use poison here – we use the dirk if we want to finish someone off.

Macbeth Or we used to – but now it's done by football.

Hamlet Football? You are the team we have been sent to play?

Macbeth Aye. And where's the rest of yours?

(Claudius and Gertrude enter SR)

Gertrude Where is that son of mine?

Birnam Well, that looks like some of the rest.

Gertrude We have been looking everywhere for you, and where do we find you?

Claudius In a drinking den.

Macbeth Excuse me – this is a respectable public house.

Claudius And you are?

Macbeth They call me, Macbeth!

(Blackout and sounds of thunder)

Beth Sorry, that always happens. We get used to it round here.

(Lights return)

Gertrude *(To Hamlet)* Why are you not at the training session?

Claudius Because he is idle.

Gertrude He can speak for himself.

Claudius He does not run, he does not tackle, he is always in two minds: to shoot or not to shoot. Hah! Why do I have him in my team, that is the question.

Gertrude He is a dead ball specialist.

Claudius He is your son – that is the only reason he is here.

Beth *(To Hamlet)* Are you going to say something, or are you always this moody? Here have another dram.

(She gives another glass of whisky to Hamlet, which he downs in one)

Hamlet *(Becoming a little slurred)* You should try the poison here – it is brilliant!

Claudius I do not need educating in poisons by you. I know all about poisons.

Duncan But do you know about football?

Gertrude He is our captain, following the sad death of my late husband.

Hamlet He killed him! He killed my dad. He poured poison in his ears.

Claudius The boy has drunk too much of your firewater. He talks nonsense.

Duncan Aye, well the only poison you'll get in your ears here is from the chanting of the crowds. By the way, I'm Duncan King – I'm the captain here.

Claudius I am Claudius, also King. King of Denmark.

Duncan Pleased to meet you. Where's the rest of your team?

Claudius They are just arriving. *(They enter)* Horatio, our goalkeeper; Yorick, who is good with his head; and Carl and Berg, probably the best substitutes in the world.

Glen They're no substitute for Glen and Morangie.

Gertrude I hear we have a neutral referee coming from England.

Beth If he's English he'll not be neutral to the Scots.

(Lady Godiva enters SR)

Duncan Hello, is this one of yours?

Claudius She is not known to me, yet.

Gertrude She had better not be known to you, ever!

Duncan *(To Godiva)* Can I help you, lassie?

Godiva Golly. Thank you, yes. I'm looking for a football match.

Duncan Then you've come to the right place. We're the lads who'll be playing.

Godiva Oh smashing!

Duncan And may I ask what your interest is?

Godiva I've been sent to referee it.

(For a moment you cannot hear a pin drop)

Duncan *(Laughing)* Nice try lassie. Now, what are you really here for?

(Godiva shows him a document)

Godiva No, really. Here's my FIFA card.

Duncan Your wha'?

Godiva They're really progressive at the Coventry Convent. Gave me time off to do the courses and everything. Jolly good fun.

Claudius We came all this way to be refereed by a woman?

Godiva Oh, I'm jolly fair. Know the off-side rule like the back of my hand.

Duncan *(Reading her card)* Godiva, Lady. What sort of a name is that?

Godiva Oh gosh – a bit OTT isn't it, the Lady bit. My husband Leo's fault really – they made him an Earl, so I became a lady. Didn't have to do anything for it – just happened.

Claudius Your husband let you become a football referee?

Godiva Glad to get me out of the house actually. Gets on with all his stuffy things in peace while I'm not there.

Claudius Stuffy things?

Godiva Oh, you know, collecting taxes, evicting tenants, flogging felons – all the usual sort of stuff that Earls do. I just get in his way. Or so he says. Just because I rode through the middle of Coventry on a horse.

Duncan So he's inflicting you on us instead.

Godiva Well, at least I'd keep my shirt on, he said.

Duncan I'm no' understanding that.

Godiva No, probably just as well. So, where is the game being played?

Claudius That is not yet decided. We, that is the Danes, would like to play it near to the town – but they, the Scotch, want to play it on a blasted heath.

Macbeth Aye, as it was foretold by the three hags.

Claudius They would be Scottish hags of course.

Macbeth They travel in time and space – they are not of this world.

Godiva Crikey, I wouldn't want to meet them on a dark night then. Well, how are we going to get over this one? Toss for it? I've got a groat in my purse.

Macbeth We must do more than toss a mere coin if we are to appease the hags.

Claudius A penalty shoot-out?

Godiva At the start of the game? Rules won't allow it.

Claudius Then I think we should forget the whole idea of a football match and have a good old-fashioned war instead. What do you say, lads?

Carl We did not bring our weapons, boss.

Berg Nor the horses.

Duncan A war sounds a good idea in that case.

Glen Aye, we're with you there boss.

Morangie Sounds like we could win this one.

Glen About six hundred to nil.

Godiva Typical boys! Come up against the tiniest problem and it's, 'let's have a fight to sort it out.' Can't you think of anything cleverer.

Macbeth Like what?

Godiva Well, at my school we used to decide who had the best argument by having each side make a speech.

Duncan We're not much good at speaking.

Godiva The find someone who is. You must both have someone who's clever with words.

Macbeth There's that fellow McGonagall. Writes the long poems.

Duncan Aye. I don't understand them, but they seem to go down well.

Godiva Does anybody write in Denmark?

Claudius Can you think of anyone, Gert?

Gertrude Difficult business writing in runes.

Hamlet *(Shaking off his hangover)* Hans Christian Andersen!

Claudius & Gertrude Who?

Hamlet Ask anyone to name a Danish writer and they say Hans Christian Andersen.

Gertrude What was that you were drinking, dear?

Godiva If you can find him, bring him on! Andersen versus McGonagall sounds good to me. And I know just the person to be judge.

Duncan Not another English person I hope.

Godiva Wait and see. Now if you chaps could tell me where the ladies loo is…

Macbeth I've no idea what you're talking about, but if you mean the midden, it tha' way. *(He points SL)*

Godiva Thank you so much. And let's all look forward to a spiffing competition.

(Close curtains)

First Interval if you are serving a 2-course meal to the audience

<u>Act I Scene 4</u> **Bard-off #1** *(Front of tabs)*

(Enter Skye Blue)

Skye Ladies and Gentlemen, let me introduce myself. I am Skye Blue of the *Mercia Mercury* in Coventry, here to report on the football and in particular how our local girl, Lady Godiva, gets on reffing her first big match. And what a needle match it has turned out to be. The Scots are needling the Danes and the Danes are needling the Scots and our mini midland lass will be there in the middle to sort it all out. If they let her.

But first, they have to decide on a venue. Will it be the city ground, or will it be the blasted heath? And to help make that choice, it is my pleasure to introduce the two national bards who will contest this important decision. In the Blue corner, weighing in with *The Tay Bridge Disaster* and other bardic gems, William Topaz McGonagall of Scotland.

(McGonagall enters SR)

And in the Red corner, famed author of the *Little Mermaid* and the *Ugly Duckling*, Hans Christian Andersen of Denmark.

(Andersen enters SL)

The rules are simplicity itself. Each bard will have one minute to make the best case for his country's choice of pitch, and at the end of this time you will hear this sound. *(Appropriate sound is heard)*

After both bards have spoken, the winner will be announced by the judge whose decision will be final. As indeed it should be considering who is doing the judging.

So without further ado, let me invite our first bard to the bar.

(McGonagall moves to the centre)

McGonagall Beautiful heath which begins just across the way
On which if I have to say my say
The best football in Scotland could be seen today
Particularly if Lady Godiva runs the line
Which will be remember'd for a very long time.

At three o'clock 'twill be a fearful sight,
Two teams there kicking out with all their might,
And probably the rain comes pouring down
And the dark clouds in the sky do seem to frown
And demons in the air are there to say
"I'll blow away the game they want to play."

But canny Scots know how to play,
And take the game to extra time and penalties I dare say.
Boreas he may loud and angry bray
And shake the heather from its roots along the way,
But see upon the heath Godiva blows the whistle for full time
Which will be remember'd for a very long time.

(McGonagall takes his bow and moves back to SR)

Skye And now I invite Mr Andersen to take the stand.

(Andersen moves to the centre)

Andersen   There once was an ugly village
With buildings all grubby and brown
And all you heard in so many words was –
Get out of town
Get out, get out, get out of town
And business was slack and the boss gave you the sack
If you laid in your eiderdown.

That poor little ugly village
Was known both far and near
But at every place they said to its face –
Get out of here
Get out, get out, get out of here
And the people came back with a waddle and a quack
And a very unhappy tear.

All through the centuries they hid themselves away

Ashamed to show their face, afraid of what others might say,
All through the centuries in their lonely clump of reed
Till a flock of Danes spied them there and very soon agreed
You're a very fine town indeed!

A town? Me a town? Ah, go on!
And they said yes, you're a town,
Take a look at yourself in the lake and you'll see
And he looked, and he saw, and he said
I am a town! Wheeeeeeee!

I'm not such an ugly village
With buildings all grubby and brown
For in fact these Danes in so many runes said
The bestest town,
the best, the best, the bestest town.

Not the sack, not so slack, but a forward and a back
And a side and a whistle and a football pitch to pack,
And a stand so noble and high
Say who's an ugly village? Not I!

(Andersen takes his bow and moves back to SL)

Skye So, you have heard both offerings and you will no doubt have your own favourite. But now it is time to invite our celebrity judge to reveal both himself and his decision. It is of course none other than that bard of bards, author of both *Mac* and *Hamlet*, and brought here from Stratford at great expense and considerable discomfort, Mr William Shakespeare.

(Shakespeare enters and moves to the centre)

May we have your comments and your decision, Mr Shakespeare.

Shakespeare So now has Hamlet fled his Elsinore
　　　　　　　　And here in Scotland with his retinues
　　　　　　　　Made plans to meet the clans in combat sore
　　　　　　　　Upon a grassy knoll which we must choose.
　　　　　　　　Should we with hags upon a heathy heath
　　　　　　　　Connive in this association dire?
　　　　　　　　How now the Danish in the town beneath
　　　　　　　　Aspiring to control both pitch and choir?
　　　　　　　　The die is cast – to be or not to be?
　　　　　　　　Observe the cursèd letter in my hand,
　　　　　　　　When opened giving authenticity
　　　　　　　　To my decision, which is final – and – *(a pause)*

> Despite the Danish fighting to the death,
> We choose the blasted heath as per Macbeth!

(Blackout and sounds of thunder)

Shakespeare Sorry! Can we have the lights back on please?

(The lights come back on)

(Shakespeare takes his applause and moves to SR)

Skye *(Coming to centre)* So there you have it ladies and gentlemen, from the mouth of the biggest bard of them all. It's ta-ta to the town and bring on the blasted heath! We'll see you there shortly for the match of the millennia.

(Exeunt)

<u>**Act I Scene 5**</u> **Witches Brew** *(Half Set)*

(We find the witches round a cauldron)

Witches Round about the cauldron go;
> In the poisoned entrails throw.
> Toad, that under the cold stone
> Days and nights has thirty-one
> Sweltered venom sleeping got,
> Boil thou first in the charmèd pot.
> Double, double, toil and trouble;
> Fire burn and cauldron bubble.

Witch 3 Is it ready yet?

(Witch 1 pulls out a wet football shirt dyed a strange colour)

Witch 1 What do you think?

Witch 2 Which team is that supposed to be?

Witch 3 None that I know of.

Witch 2 Perhaps we're using the wrong spell.

Witch 1 We're using the one in the book.

Witch 3 Aye, but what does the book know about football?

Witch 2 Never say dye. Let's try some of those chants the Doctor taught us.

Witch 1 Do you remember them?

Witch 2 No, I don't.

Witch 3 Perhaps the audience can help us. Do you know any football chants?

Witch 2 Preferably clean ones!

(Business with the audience singing chants)

(Witch 1 eventually pulls out a red shirt and a blue one)

Witch 1 Is that better?

Witch 2 *(Taking the red one)* Denmark.

Witch 3 *(Taking the blue one)* Scotland.

Witch 1 So, now we've got it right we can make more of those for the rest of the teams.

Witch 2 What about the referee?

Witch 3 She can't wear nothing, can she?

(Business with the audience – oh yes she can, etc)

Witch 1 I'll make her a natty little black number. Very slimming.

Witch 2 Slimming – ooh!

Witch 3 Can you make one for us too?

Witch 1 You're supposed to be bewitching not Beyoncé.

Witch 2 They'll need touch judges.

Witch 3 We can run the line.

Witch 1 Oh my! I can see the headline now – 'Hitch as Kitsch Witch triggers Glitch on the Pitch.' But against my better judgement ...

Witch 2 You will, won't you.

Witch 1 *(Sighs, then)*
    Back to the cauldron, back to the pot –
    black's the colour for this lot.

(Curtains begin to close on them as they resume their chanting)

    Fillet of a fenny snake,
    In the cauldron boil and bake;
    Eye of newt and toe of frog,
    Wool of bat and tongue of dog,

> Adder's fork and blind-worm's sting,
> Lizard's leg and owlet's wing,
> For a charm of powerful trouble,
> Like a hell-broth boil and bubble.
> Double, double, toil and trouble;
> Fire burn and cauldron bubble.

Act I Scene 6 On the field – teams in training *(Full Set)*

(We start front of tabs while scene behind is set)

(Polonius and Ophelia enter DSR)

Polonius It is really very simple. A player is in an offside position if he is nearer to his opponents' goal line than both the ball and the second last opponent. I cannot see why you should find that difficult.

Ophelia The second last opponent?

Polonius The second last opponent.

Ophelia How can you have a second last opponent? You can only have one last opponent, otherwise he is not the last.

Polonius The second last is the one before the last.

Ophelia Then why not say so? Second last is confusing.

Polonius Anyway, your job does not need you to know the rules of football – you just keep the players fit and we shall do the rest.

Ophelia That is easier said than done. Out here on some god-forsaken waste ground…

Polonius Officially it is a blasted heath.

Ophelia Blasted heath, whatever. No rest room, no running water…

Polonius It is only 1040 dear – you can't expect running water this early.

Ophelia Pardon me, but it is past noon and I still see no sign of it.

Polonius I was referring to the year, not the time.

Ophelia So I suppose we shall have no antiseptics or analgesics either.

Polonius I beg your pardon?

Ophelia You may know the offside rule, but you obviously do not know much about medical matters.

29

Polonius I have started to feel very old since the turn of the millennium. I knew nothing would work in the old way as soon as the year had four figures in it.

Ophelia We are in the 11th century now, dad. You do not want to get left behind.

Polonius No? I suppose not. Now then, where is that blasted field?

Ophelia I believe it is on the other side of these drooping drapes.

(The curtains open on cue – the blasted heath is revealed)

Polonius This is a football pitch?

Ophelia So I am told.

Polonius Thor's bones! Has it come to this?

Ophelia It is the same for both sides.

Polonius They have home advantage.

Ophelia We are the Great Danes, remember? We eat Scotties for lunch.

Polonius They go for the ankles though. The ref will have to look out for that. I shall make sure to tell him.

Ophelia Her.

Polonius Pardon?

Ophelia The ref is a her.

Polonius Now I really do feel past it.

Ophelia You can still tell her.

Polonius Yes, but probably not much. Where has our team got to? – we need all the practice we can get on this alien turf.

Ophelia Shall I give them a call?

Polonius You tease me, daughter. Or has this century produced a device for speaking over long distances that I have not heard of?

Ophelia No, only the old device. *(Yells offstage, or whistles if able)* Here, you lot – get a move on!

(The Danish team drifts on from SR: Claudius, Hamlet, Horatio, Yorick, Carl & Berg along with Gertrude)

Claudius Can you not teach your daughter some respect, Polonius?

Gertrude No daughter of mine would be allowed to shout like that.

Polonius You have no daughter, Gertrude. Only a son with a partiality for small cheroot cigars.

Ophelia When he can get them, eh Hammie?

Gertrude And do not call him Hammie. It makes him sound like a small rodent.

Ophelia I had heard he was more like a rabbit, if you know what I mean.

Polonius I very much hope we do not know what you mean!

Ophelia Oh, Hammie and me were hanging out for a while you know. *(To Hamlet)* Weren't we, Hammie?

Hamlet Ophelia, do you have to bring that up? It was a long time ago.

Ophelia Memorable though.

Polonius *(Clears throat)* May we get to the matter in hand…

Ophelia That is what Hammie used to say.

Polonius …and start doing a work-out for this wretched football match. Claudius, you are the captain – can you get your team working please.

Claudius Right, this way team. We shall do some warm-ups over there.

(The Danish team moves off SL)

Gertrude *(To Ophelia)* And if you are thinking doing any physiotherapy on my Hammie during this match you can think again.

Ophelia All right, I shall just leave him to stiffen up if you would prefer.

Gertrude Really, young girls today! *(She follows the team off)*

Polonius Not very clever getting on the wrong side of the Queen, my girl. You might rue the day.

(Enter Skye and Godiva)

Skye Hello there. Is this the right place for the football match?

Polonius It is the selected place. Whether or not it is the right place is another matter.

Ophelia Do not listen to dad – he is in the dumps today. Hi, I am Feely – who are you?

Skye Skye Blue, news. What did you say your name was again?

Ophelia It is Ophelia really, but everyone calls me Feely. Except for dad, that is.

Polonius Do not go along with all this new millennium stuff. Feely indeed! It will be Touchy Feely next, and then what?

Skye *(Interested)* Indeed. Um, may I introduce you to Lady Godiva.

Godiva *(Holds out her hand to Polonius)* Jolly pleased to meet you.

Polonius *(Taking hers)* And I you, madam. Nice to take part in a good old-fashioned greeting for once. You are obviously of the old school.

Godiva Golly, not so much of the old I should hope.

Polonius Pardon me – I did not mean to imply – not your age, you understand, just your manners. Every inch a Lady. And may I ask for what reason you grace us with your presence.

Skye She's the match referee.

Polonius I can see you are the wit of the newsroom, Mr Skye.

Godiva No, sorry to blow your impression of me out of the window, but I am actually the referee.

Ophelia Wicked!

Polonius Ophelia, please restrain yourself! *(To Godiva, slowly)* You are the referee? *(Blinks)* Excuse me, I think it is time for my slippers and bed. You youngsters can take over – well, it looks like you are taking over already. New millennium indeed! *(He exits SL)*

Godiva Oh dear – he doesn't sound happy.

Ophelia Oh do not mind him – he enjoys being miserable, the old donkey! So, the ref, eh? Come far?

Skye We're from Coventry.

Ophelia We are from Elsinore. Danish.

Skye I know – we read the pre-match notes.

Ophelia Yes, of course.

Skye You're a long way from home.

Ophelia Yes, we are. It is across the sea, Denmark.

Skye Yes, I know. A longboat ride away.

Ophelia A longboat – yes, that is a good joke.

Godiva I'm sorry to butt in and all that, but shouldn't we be inspecting the pitch or something?

Skye Sorry Golly – I was on another planet for a moment there.

Ophelia Golly?

Godiva Oh it's my wretched nickname – I suppose because I'm always saying 'Golly'!

Ophelia *(To Skye)* On nickname terms with the ref then, are we?

Skye Oh Golly and I go back a long way.

Ophelia Yes, all the way back to Coventry why don't you.

(Enter Hamlet from SL)

Hamlet Feely, we are all waiting for you. Are you coming or not?

Skye *(To Ophelia)* On nickname terms with the Prince then, are we?

Ophelia Oh Hammie and I …

Skye …go back a long way. Yes.

Ophelia We were just getting to know the referee.

Hamlet We have met. She arranged for us to play on this blasted pitch.

Godiva Tut tut – language! And that's not fair. It was determined by the bards.

Hamlet Your idea though.

Godiva You boys didn't seem to be coming up with a better one. You'd have started chopping off bits of each other's anatomy again if I hadn't been there. That wouldn't have done you much good, would it?

Ophelia Oh, I am not sure anyone would have noticed with Hammie.

Hamlet Ophelia, please. It was years ago and I think I have grown up since then.

Ophelia Enough said! We shall see how much you have grown up when I get you on the massage table.

(Ophelia heads for exit SL)

Skye Just a minute – I'll come with you. I need a piece for the morning press.

(Skye follows Ophelia heads off SL)

Hamlet   Sorry about that. Never at my best when Feely is around.

Godiva   Too much touchy in the past?

Hamlet   Someone should write a play about it.

Godiva   Don't suppose anyone will get round to writing a play about me.

Hamlet   You should be glad. They only write plays when your life has been a drama. Not much to tell about a convent girl I imagine.

Godiva   S'pose not. There was the time I rode naked through the town. But I don't suppose that's anything exceptional for convent girls.

Hamlet   I do not know any convent girls.

Godiva   Perhaps you should.

Hamlet   You have a husband back home.

Godiva   He's just an Earl. They say you're a Prince.

Hamlet   I should be a King.

Godiva   Like Claudius.

Hamlet   Instead of Claudius the poisoner.

Godiva   Golly, I'd like to be a fly on the wall in your team talks.

Hamlet   I am just waiting my moment to strike. When his defences are down.

Godiva   Make sure you're not offside when you do. I might have to card you.

Hamlet   Red carded by a Lady. Might even be worth it.

(Enter the witches SR, in their new black strip, not entirely to their liking)

Witch 1   Ah, there you are ref. I've brought your linesmen.

Witch 2   Are you canoodling with the opposition there?

Hamlet   Just checking up on the rules of engagement. Captain's orders.

Witch 3   Don't miss out on your warm-up. Ye don't want to pull a muscle now.

(Hamlet exits SL)

Witch 2   If you ask me he was warming up more than a muscle. If I knew how to spell it I'd say it was fraternisation.

Witch 3 Don't talk to me about spell. I think we got our eye of newt and toe of frog mixed up. What an outfit!

Witch 1 Stop snittering there. They're perfectly good outfits. And we've brought this one for you, ref.

Godiva Crickey, do I have to wear that?

Witch 1 Can't have you in the buff, can we!

Godiva Not since I had the hair cut shorter, no.

Witch 1 So off you go and get changed – make sure it fits and covers the bits. These two will help you. I'm sure there's a bush somewhere.

(Godiva and the two witches exit SL)

So the Danes are out there, looking fit even if their minds aren't on the job. Oh dear, here come the Scots!

*(The Scottish team staggers on singing tunelessly from SR:
Duncan, Macbeth, Banquo, Birnam, Glen & Morangie)*

Banquo Are we there yet?

Witch 1 Aye, you're here. Which one of you's sober enough to be in charge?

Birnam Witch one? That's you isn't it? It says so in the script. Witch One.

Banquo That makes you in charge.

Witch 1 No way! Duncan. Duncan King! You're team's wrecked.

Duncan We're merry.

Glen Duncan and his merry men!

Morangie Going to win the cup again!

Witch 1 You're not going to win a thimble in that state. The Danes are fighting fit and you turn up roaring drunk.

Banquo 'Sonly the warm up. Match isn't for hours yet.

Birnam Hours and hours …

Banquo …and hours and hours.

(They lean against each other and start to sing a football chant)

Witch 1 Can't any of you hold your drink?

(Duncan, Glen and Morangie turn to have a pee backstage)

Apparently not. You're very quiet, Mac.

Macbeth So foul and fair a day I have not seen.

Witch 1 Blind drunk – I thought so.

(Enter Beth SR)

Beth Wha' the hell's going on here?

Witch 1 I think hell is about to leave – exit Witch One into hell's gate. It should be quieter there!

(Witch 1 exits in appropriate direction)

Beth It's those Danes – they've spiked your drinks with lager.

Macbeth Time and the hour runs through the roughest day.

Beth You're talking gibberish man Mac. How much did you drink?

Macbeth I drink to the general joy.

Beth Look me in the eye.

Macbeth Let not light see my black and deep desires

Beth I don't know who writes your lines, but they're rubbish.

(The rest of the team are sobering up)

So are you fit to play now?

Duncan We'll do.

Beth Aye, do what though?

Banquo Slay the Danes.

Birnam No problem.

Glen Five nil by half time.

Morangie Bring them on!

Macbeth Birnam Wood shall come against them.

Birnam Aye, and the rest of you.

Beth Then screw your courage to the sticking-place, and we'll not fail.

Banquo Wha' does that mean?

Beth I've no idea, but it sounds good – and the Danes won't understand it either.   *(All exit SL as the curtain falls)*

<u>**Act I Scene 7**</u> **Supporters' Views** *(Front of Tabs)*

(Skye enters SR with microphone)

Skye We're testing the atmosphere before the big international match here in Scotland today, and I'd just like to catch the comments of some of the supporters for you back home in Mercia.

(Enter SL, Bottom the Weaver with ass's head)

May I ask you, sir, who you'll be supporting today?

Bottom Don't be an ass!

Skye I'm sorry. I *ass*umed even an *ass* had *a cer*tain point of view.

Bottom Yes. Through the mouth *[or whatever the costume dictates]* at the moment.

Skye Then it was a false *ass*umption?

Bottom It's a false head. I'm looking for the fairy queen who fixed it on me.

Skye I imagine you'll find him backstage. Good luck.

(Bottom exits SR as Puck enters SL with besom)

So, no dice with the donkey. Ah, who have we here? Looks like mischief to me. Have you time for a few words?

Puck The hungry lion roars.

Skye Er, I imagine it does. But what about the football international?

Puck I'll put a girdle round about the earth in forty minutes. Broooom!

Skye I suppose that's international enough. Are you attending the match before you fly off?

Puck I am sent with broom before, to sweep the dust behind the door.

(Puck exits SR on broom as Malvolio enters SL with yellow garters)

Skye So the changing rooms will be clean then. Well thank you for those very few words. Ah – who is this majestic-looking gentleman? We should at least get some sense from him. Good day sir.

Malvolio Good day to you.

Skye Would you care to share your thoughts on today's football match?

Malvolio I marvel you take delight in such a barren rascally business.

Skye You don't approve then?

Malvolio Are you mad, or what are you? Have you no wit, manners, nor honesty, but to gabble like tinkers at this so-called sport?

Skye You're not wearing your team colours then?

Malvolio I must be round with you. Though yellow in my legs I am not afraid of greatness.

(Malvolio exits SR as Henry V enters SL in armour)

Skye Well, I'm sure some of our listeners will know what you're talking about. I have to say, these interviews are not going entirely the way I had hoped they would. Good heavens, what's this? – a man from the future. Do they play football in your times, sire?

King Henry It is forbidden. Men must attend their butts to practice their archery in their leisure time.

Skye A different sort of shooting skill.

King Henry Kicking a pig's bladder will not prevent the French and the Scots from invading us. Only the longbow will do that. Did football save England in 1066?

Skye 1066? We haven't got there yet. It's 26 years away. What happens then?

King Henry Prepare for Domesday – I will say no more – I have said too much already. *(He prepares to exit SR)*

Skye Domesday? Sounds a bit final.

King Henry On the other hand I am told that 1966 will be a year in which football does save the country. But personally I'd stick to the longbow.

(Henry V exits SR as Cleopatra enters SL with asp)

Skye Twenty-six years before what? Should I renew my insurance? Ah now, we all know who this lady is. Hi Cleo.

Cleopatra I am sick and sullen.

Skye Oh dear. Well, nothing like a nice game of football to cheer you up, eh?

Cleopatra Dost thou not see my baby at my breast?

Skye Well, to be honest I was trying not to look – but now you mention it … it's a fine asp you have there.

Cleopatra Many have admired it throughout Egypt.

Skye I'm sure they have – it beggars all description – now, about football …

Cleopatra Anthony said I was his goal.

Skye What was the final result?

Cleopatra A score draw, I think he called it. Does that mean anything to you?

Skye I'd play for a score draw with you any day.

Cleopatra Wouldn't it hurt my asp?

Skye Not if your Libero's working well.

Cleopatra My Libero?

Skye Your centre back.

Cleopatra I don't understand. You're not trying to pull a fast one on me, are you? Two Caesars tried that and look where it got them.

Skye Immortalised.

Cleopatra Well, yes, but don't bank on the same thing happening to you sonny. Right, we're off for a light bite.

(Cleopatra exits SR as Romeo & Juliet enter SL smooching)

Skye There's no casting *asp*ersions on her. Oh-ho – here comes double trouble.

Juliet *(To Romeo)* Wherefore art thou Romeo?

Romeo *(To Juliet)* What's in a name? Rose by any other name would smell the same.

Juliet Rose? I'll say! Have you been downwind of her? BO or what!

Romeo I agree – personal hygiene was never her strong point.

Juliet You didn't fancy her, did you?

Romeo It was my parents – you know how it is. Right family, right connections, etc, etc.

Juliet Mine too. My father said that if I so much as talked to you he'd emasculate you. What does that mean?

Romeo Does he own a great big pair of iron things that look like tongs with knobs on?

Juliet Yes, he keeps them above the fireplace. And he's marked notches on the wall beside them.

Romeo How many boyfriends have you had?

Juliet 'Bout six.

Romeo And how many notches on the wall?

Juliet 'Bout six.

Romeo You know, I might give Rose another try. If I wear a mask it might not be so bad.

Skye Excuse me – I can see you're busy but …

Romeo No, suddenly I don't think we're busy at all.

Juliet Says who?

Skye Then perhaps you'd like to give me your views on football?

Romeo Ah, the beautiful game.

Juliet You talking about Rose again? Beautiful game? She might be game but she's never beautiful.

Romeo Listen Jules, this is boys' talk, right?

Juliet Oooh, listen to Mr Top Gear.

Skye Did you know there's a match on today, just along the track?

Romeo Who's playing?

Juliet Hey, what happened to the romantic walk along the coast?

Skye Big names – Scotland v Denmark – not to be missed.

Romeo Sounds interesting.

Skye You may be coming then?

Juliet If he is, you can tear up the script of the most romantic love story in the world.

Romeo But at least I won't die at the end of it.

Juliet Oh, so my love's not worth dying for then?

Romeo It always was a bit of a downer to be honest.

Juliet I die too.

Romeo Yeah, but girls like that kind of slushy ending – me, I've never really taken to it.

Juliet I might just die anyway, of a broken heart.

Romeo That's up to you, Jules. *(To Skye)* How much are tickets for the match?

Skye Can't grumble at a groat a piece can you?

Romeo I may be back.

Juliet With a dagger in his chest!

(Romeo & Juliet exit SR still bickering)

Skye So it's a matter of: 'He can bring Rose with her high stench woes, but don't bring Julie.' Time we moved swiftly on, I think. Let's see how training is going.

Act I Scene 8 In the Gym *(Full Set)*

We observe various characters working out in the gym to appropriate music. Mime where necessary. Use what resources you have and work to the strengths of your actors

Suggestions:—

Witches 2 and 3 on gym bikes. Godiva joins them on a third bike and is obviously fitter.

The two teams do weight-lifting, jogging, stretching or whatever else can be brought to stage.

Have some 'head to head' competitions, and let the women generally out-perform the men to the distress of the latter

Polonius does little, and that grudgingly.

At the end all except the Scottish team exit.

Macbeth 'I dare do all that may become a man' – but this wasn't part of the agreement.

Glen Tell me about it!

Morangie Who's idea was it anyway.

Duncan Personally, I blame it on that young woman from Coventry. What right has she got to come up here all prissy and start ordering us about. We're grown men.

Banquo *(Mimicking)* Golly Godiva.

Birnam More like, God I've a nerve!

Macbeth How can we play a good game when she's shattered us. It's a conspiracy.

Glen Mind you, she put the Danes through it too!

Morangie Aye, but they're fitter than us. They had to row across the sea to get here.

Banquo In that case we need to make them unfit.

Birnam To even it up like.

Duncan Good idea. But how?

Glen We could ask the witches to put a spell on them.

Morangie Make them into toads, or something.

Duncan I somehow think the public would notice that, and I don't trust them and their spells anyway. We just need to slow them down a bit.

Macbeth Food poisoning. That would slow them down.

Glen Or speed them up in the other direction!

Morangie Nasty!

Banquo Have you seen what they eat? Bits of cold meat on slices of toast. That's no meal!

Birnam Not like a good wholesome plate of thick porridge. I wonder they live on what they eat.

Macbeth That's it! We give them porridge. They won't be used to the weight of it.

Duncan They wouldn't eat it if we gave it to them.

Glen That drink of theirs though – that's got to be possibly the worst drink in the world.

Morangie Enough of that should weigh them down.

Duncan So we need a plan – a cunning plan. Who's good at cunning?

Banquo, Birnam, Glen & Morangie Macbeth!

(Blackout and sounds of thunder)

Duncan Oh come on – it's beyond a joke now.

(Lights return)

42

Duncan Thank you.

Macbeth I'll need an interval to think of something.

Duncan Then an interval is what ye'll get. There's no art to find the mind's construction in the face.

Macbeth Wha' does tha' mean?

Duncan No idea. Come on, let's go and have a wee dram. Last one to the bar buys the round.

They all rush to exit as the curtains close

*** INTERVAL ***

<u>**Act II Scene 1**</u> **Polonius explains the situation** *(Front of Tabs)*

(Polonius enters.)

Polonius Now forgive me if I seem a little pre-millennium but – I do not know about you – but I am having a little difficulty in understanding quite what is going on here. Indulge me a little if you would and let me think out loud to see if we can make head or tail of it. Speaking of which I gather they intend to toss a groat to see who plays from which wretched end of the blasted heath. Incredible.

But I digress – which sadly is a constant failing of mine. Now where was I? I seem to have lost – ah yes! – the plot.

You may be more familiar than I with all this travelling in time and space business – well, you could not be less familiar as I have lived my entire life as a fictional character in a fusty old castle in Denmark. I am told that I am now living, if you will, in what the author intriguingly calls a 'parallel universe'. I believe this is a device which allows authors the excuse to write whatever they like whether it makes sense or not, and leaves the likes of you and me to puzzle it out.

That man Shakespeare started it all of course, but I suppose I should not complain about him or I would not be here! Perhaps some of you might think that would be a good thing. I cannot really disagree with you. The number of clichés he puts into his writing! 'To be or not to be' – 'now is the winter of our discontent' – you know the sort of stuff. One could not get away with it now.

However, we are where we are – wherever that is – and now we must move on. Yes. I think that is all I have to say. Not sure it makes any more sense that it did before I started droning on really. Ah well, let us 'cut to the chase' as they say, as see if the second half makes any more sense than the first. Though personally I am not hopeful.

(Polonius exits)

Act II Scene 2 **Still in the Pub** *(Full Set)*

The pub is still populated with Scottish revellers

A 'bottle xylophone' is made of party-filled bottles of scotch – business – whichever of your Scottish team actors are capable play tunes on it.

Duncan Give me 'Scotland the Brave'.

(Somebody manages to play it, or something like it)

Banquo Pity we had to drink so much whisky to tune the bottles.

Birnam Aye, and some of them went wrong so we had to start over again.

Duncan Good result though. Now do 'Speed Bonny Boat'.

Banquo That might be in a different key, Dunc.

Birnam Then we'll have to tune them again again.

Duncan Well, so be it!

Macbeth Stand to attention – the wife's arrived!

(Enter Beth SR)

Beth Someone said there was a ceilidh going on here, but I see it's just you.

Duncan Are ye casting nasturtiums on our playing?

Beth You're even worse at music than you are at football, and that's saying something.

Duncan You're the team manager – you're supposed to be encouraging us.

Beth I'm supposed to be telling you that the opposition are about to walk in through that door, and you'd better be ready with your plan because if it doesn't work you're certainly not going to beat them on the pitch in that condition. Savvy?

Macbeth I'd listen to her Duncan – she's a murderer when she's roused.

The Danish enter from SR: Claudius, Gertrude, Hamlet, Horatio, Yorick, Carl & Berg – they each carry a bottle of Carlsberg.

Gertrude I am told we have been challenged to be a pre-match competition.

Beth Aye.

Gertrude But we have not been told what is the competition.

Macbeth It's just a bit of fun. Nothing serious.

Gertrude You remind me of my Hamlet – he also says 'nothing serious' one minute and the next you find people dying all over the place.

Hamlet Since when?

Gertrude Read the script that nice Mr Shakespeare gave you.

Claudius So what is this 'bit of fun'?

Beth It's a music competition.

Horatio Music? *(To Claudius)* Do Danes do music?

Yorick Do the Scots? Have you ever heard bagpipes?

Beth We're no' using the bagpipes. Tha' would be unfair.

Gertrude A fair competition – what a novelty! Where is the catch?

Macbeth No catch. You make your own instrument – and then play it. The best performance wins.

Carl Make an instrument?

Berg Out of what?

Beth The answer is in your hands.

Carl What do you mean?…

Berg … in our hands?

Beth The bottles. Let's see if you can get a tune out of them.

Horatio Just like that?

Macbeth Just like that.

(They strike the bottles with daggers, changing positions to get a 7-note scale)

Gertrude You did not think we could do it, did you?

Duncan Was that your performance?

Horatio Let me see you do better.

Duncan *(To his team)* Have you drunk that line of bottles into tune yet?

Banquo What key was it again? *(Looking at Birnam flat out on the floor)* He's B flat anyway.

Beth I'll give you something B sharp soon. See – like I said, you're just a team of losers.

Duncan We've got a lot of bottle though.

Gertrude *(To Beth)* That is men for you, dear. All talk and no performance.

Beth Is your Dane not great then?

Gertrude He is a dog when he is roused! How is your wee Scottie?

Beth He's got a bite to him.

Gertrude *(Looking at Macbeth)* Right now I would say he could not bite a bread pudding.

Beth Just as well for you, then – you won't get bitten.

Gertrude Was it your face they modelled the haggis on?

Beth It'll be your guts we'll stuff for the next one!

  (Enter Polonius and Ophelia just in time to stop a brawl ensuing)

Polonius How are we all getting on then?

Claudius We are having a 'bit of fun,' or so I am told. The Scots seem to do all their fighting indoors.

Duncan Is that right? Well I don't suppose you have any indoorses to fight in.

Polonius I thought we were preparing for a football match.

Duncan Aye, so we are – if we can stop the women from taking over.

Ophelia The referee says she is ready for you now.

Claudius Duncan, my friend, they've already taken over.

Duncan Right. Mac, better get the team together.

Macbeth What's this? Some sort of inspection?

Claudius Looks like it.

Ophelia Offkit.

Macbeth Pardon?

Ophelia The referee wants to inspect your kit.

Duncan Sounds a bit personal to me.

Macbeth Aye, especially with the wife watching.

Beth You've nothing to show.

Gertrude Either of you.

Ophelia Dream on. She wants to look at the kit you will be wearing. If you have any.

Polonius So if you would all be so kind as to make your way to the field of combat…

Claudius The blasted heath…

Polonius …with your kit on, we can begin the game.

The two teams exit leaving Polonius, Ophelia, Beth & Gertrude on stage

Beth Let battle commence!

Gertrude You can do better than that, can't you?

Beth Better than what?

Gertrude "Let battle commence". Not very Shakespearean.

Beth Out, damned spot! out, I say!

Gertrude The lady doth protest too much, methinks.

Polonius This above all – to thine ownself be true;
And it must follow, as the night the day,
Thou canst not then be false to any man.

Ophelia Or woman, dad. Come on, let us get to the pitch.

Exeunt

Act II Scene 3 Bard-off #2 *(Ends Front of Tabs)*

Enter Will McGonagall and Hans Christian Andersen from opposite sides

McGonagall Did ye hear that, Mr Andersen? They were quoting the bard!

Andersen That is our job, Mr McGonagall.

McGonagall Indeed it is, Mr Andersen. We are usurped.

Andersen Barred from our job.

McGonagall Bard is our job.

Andersen Ready for a bard-off then, Mr McGonagall.

McGonagall I most certainly am, Mr Andersen.

> *They move forward, the curtain closes behind them*

Andersen The play's the thing.

McGonagall Fair is foul, and foul is fair.

Andersen Frailty, thy name is woman!

McGonagall Stars, hide your fires!
> Let not light see my black and deep desires.

Andersen O, That this too too solid flesh would melt.

McGonagall Yet do I fear thy nature;
> It is too full o' the milk of human kindness.

Andersen Neither a borrower nor a lender be.

McGonagall Screw your courage to the sticking-place.

Andersen Something is rotten in the state of Denmark.

McGonagall Fill me from the crown to the toe, top-full
> Of direst cruelty; make thick my blood.

Andersen There are more things in heaven and earth, Horatio,
> Than are dreamt of in your philosophy.

McGonagall Is this a dagger which I see before me?

Andersen To be, or not to be, — that is the question.

McGonagall The way to dusty death.

Andersen Alas! poor Yorick.

McGonagall All our yesterdays have lighted fools!

Andersen And flights of angels sing thee to thy rest.

> *They put their fingers to their lips for quiet, and tiptoe off*

<u>Act II Scene 4</u> **Pre-match build-up** *(Half Set)*

Skye Blue found on set with microphone

Skye And you join us at a critical moment in the build-up to this inter-national between the Scottish Players and the Hamlet Rovers. As I speak, the teams are getting their final briefing from their coaches. The Scots have home advantage on the blasted heath, but the Danes are used to playing away from home and take no prisoners. Any minute now they will appear from the dressing rooms and …

Lady Godiva enters SR with ball in a very feminine black referee's outfit

Oh my God-iva!

Godiva You've a what?

Skye This isn't Coventry, you know, Golly.

Godiva You disapprove?

Skye It doesn't leave much to the imagination.

Godiva I could go the full Coventry.

Skye Not recommended in this climate. And anyway, where would you keep your notebook?

Godiva Good point. Shouldn't you be talking into that microphone?

Skye Right. *(To the microphone)* The referee is outstanding on the pitch. She's looking good, and hard at the touchlines. And here come the other match officials.

Enter Witches 2 & 3 in their black strip

You don't have to ask 'which is which?' – the answer is, both of them!

Witch 2 *(To Godiva)* How come you end up looking like that and we end up looking like this?

Godiva Pot luck?

Witch 3 Pah! It's that Morag – she had it in for us. You got the 'charm of powerful trouble,' and we got the 'hell-broth boil and bubble'.

Skye Well, ladies, are you ready for the match to begin?

Witch 2 Bring 'em out!

Witch 3 Bring 'em on!

(Witches exit; Beth and Polonius enter)

Skye   Let's have quick word with the two team managers. *(To Beth)* Mrs MacB, how will your Scottish team perform today?

Beth   If you can look into the seeds of time, and say which grain will grow, and which will not, speak.

Skye   I see, I think. *(To Polonius)* And Mr Polonius, what do you think about your Danish team?

Polonius   Neither a follower nor defender be.

Skye   Uh-huh. Well, I suppose they do say 'fair is foul, and foul is fair,' so let's see how the match pans out.

> *The curtains open to reveal the Blasted Heath*

Act II Scene 5 The Match *(Full Set)*

> *Witch 1 and Gertrude are on stage, dressed as cheer-leaders*

Witch 1   Rah, Rah, hear our chant,
            Scots are great and Danes just aren't.

Gertrude   Ya, Ya, yes we are,
            With our boats we travel far.

Witch 1   Hey, Hey, what we say,
            You're not using boats today.

Skye   Here come the teams!

> *The teams enter to 'Match of the Day' music and line up*
> *so that there could be 11 in each side if you could see into the wings!*

Scottish team: Beth, Duncan, Macbeth, Banquo, Birnam, Glen, Morangie
Danish team: Polonius, Ophelia, Claudius, Horatio, Yorick, Carl, Berg
Between them: Witch 2, Godiva, Witch 3

Skye   And the anthems.

Scottish Team: *Sing "I would walk 500 miles"*

Danish Team: *Sing "There is nothing like a Dane!"*

> *Godiva blows her whistle and summons the team captains*
> *Duncan and Claudius for the toss*

Godiva   Now chaps, I want a good clean fight, no holding, no biting, no punching below the belt. Understood, yah?

Duncan & Claudius Yes Miss!

Godiva The coin we are using today is Pegasus, a Roman Sestertius last used in the game between Gaul and the Jutes of Kent. This is its fifth appearance in the pan-European league since the start of the millennium. Heads Scots, tails Danes. Are you ready?

Duncan & Claudius Yes Miss!

Godiva Jolly good. *(She tosses the coin)* Tails! Danes.

Claudius We'll play with the wind in our tails.

Duncan Ye'll have more than that in your tails by the end.

Teams go offstage (Scots SR, Danes SL) except for Hamlet, Macbeth Witches 2 & 3 and Godiva. Godiva places the ball, checks her watch and her lineswitches, and blows her whistle for kick-off.

Macbeth kicks the ball back to where his team is, and the match begins.

Match to be choreographed!! Scots win

Act II Scene 6 **Reviewing the Consequences** *(Front of Tabs)*

Polonius enters

Polonius Well that is all over, thank goodness. I cannot say I am sorry. Not my bag, as they say these days. Be glad to get back on the boat. But sadly they will not let us go. Will not let us go – can you imagine that? Just a few generations ago we were the feared Vikings who raped and pillaged where we would. Not saying that was reasonable behaviour, mind you, but that was how it was. And now, we cannot even put up a fight when our boats are requisitioned by the authorities. And why have they taken them? Because we have not 'coughed up' for a trophy. I did not see it in the small print, but apparently the losers have to present a trophy to the winners. And we did not bring one with us. Well, why would we? It is not in the script. So now we are stuck here until someone comes up with a solution.

The Witches enter, back in witch costumes

Witch 1 Weell, if it isna Polonius the Posh.

Witch 2 The doleful Dane…

Witch 3 …deliberating on his downfall.

Polonius Cease your caterwauling, hags! I imagine you had no small part in the victory.

51

Witch 1 Aye, you could say that.

Witch 2 You did say that.

Witch 3 And it's true.

Witch 1 Hubble, bubble, toil and trouble.

Witch 2 We were going to win the double.

Witch 3 With a team drawn from the lees
Of William Shakespeare's tragedies.

Witch 1 And we did it!

Polonius Congratulations.

Witch 2 You could say it like you mean it.

Polonius No, I could not.

Witch 3 Oh, come on Polony.

Polonius I am not a sausage. And why should I congratulate you 'like I mean it'? Your people are holding us to ransom. All for the sake of a tin cup.

Witch 1 A tin cup?

Polonius Well, a cup of some sort – I suppose it does not have to be tin.

Witch 2 Ah, Morag, remember the Doctor?

Witch 1 Who?

Witch 2 That's the one. He was telling us of the Danes and their most famous export.

Witch 3 They've just been here drinking it.

Witch 2 No, far more famous than that.

Polonius Ladies, you are losing me. Though I confess that is not difficult these days.

Witch 1 Aye, Kirsty, I remember what you're talking about now. That might be an answer to Polony's problem.

Polonius I am not P...

Witch 2 We can sort it for you. Just wait here a minute – we have an engagement with a telephone box.

Polonius A what?

Witch 3 Don't worry – something from the new millennium – you wouldn't understand.

The witches exit

Polonius Am I getting old, or is the world accelerating past me? Ah well, let us hope this doctor has a cure. I think I need a drink. Would you care to follow me to the bar? *(Exits)*

Act II Scene 7 Back in the Pub *(Full Set)*

The Scots are in a joyous group SL (Macbeth, Duncan, Banquo, Birnam, Glen & Morangie) and the Danes are in a dismal group SR (Hamlet, Claudius, Horatio, Yorick, Carl & Berg)

Glen Are you going to tell us a story again, Mac.

Morangie Aye, like last time. About the weird women.

Macbeth Not so weird now, eh? They won us the match.

Duncan But where's the trophy? We want the trophy.

All Scots *(chant)* Trophy – trophy – trophy…

Claudius Chant all you like – you would never win on a decent pitch.

Hamlet Come to Denmark and see how you do. It will be a slaughter.

Horatio It always is at the end of play in Elsinore.

Yorick Alas.

Carl Poor Yorick!

Berg Where be your flashes of merriment now?

Yorick Piss off!

(Gertrude and Ophelia enter SR)

Gertrude Did I hear that correctly?

Claudius You did. Yorick is in his cups.

Ophelia In his cups?

Hamlet That is bardic for inebriated, Feely. We are all in our cups because we have not got a cup.

Ophelia Poor Hammie. Did that nice Golly not let you win the match then?

Gertrude That will do, Ophelia. I am sure they all did their best.

Horatio Even if Hamlet did refuse to pass to Claudius for the whole match.

Gertrude They have issues to resolve off-pitch. We shall work on it.

Ophelia That sounds ominous. Better watch your back, Hammie.

(Beth enters SR)

Beth Where are my battling boys then? Moving Birnam Wood was a master stroke, don't you think?

Macbeth Aye, they weren't expecting that. And Banquo sped like a ghost through the opposition.

Banquo They thought I was one of theirs.

Ophelia I suppose you think that is in the spirit of the game.

(Godiva and Skye enter DS)

Ophelia *(Noticing)* Still here? I thought we had sent you to Coventry.

Skye Just need a few words to wrap up the report…

Ophelia I will give you a very few words. Go away!

Skye Perhaps from the team captain?

Claudius Go away.

Beth You see? They're bad losers.

Skye What's your take on the game then?

Beth Brilliant! It'll go down in history as the battle of the Blasted Heath.

Macbeth Winner takes all.

All Scots *(chant)* Trophy – trophy – trophy…

Duncan Give us our trophy!

All Scots *(chant)* Trophy – trophy – trophy…

(Polonius enters)

Polonius Calm down, calm down. You shall have your trophy.

(The three witches enter SL with Lego trophy)

Witch 1 Ta-rah!

Witch 2 Ta-rah!

Witch 3 Ta-rah!

Witch 1 With a little help from a Doctor…

Witch 2 … Who

Witch 3 … gave us a clue…

Witch 2 … as to what we should do.

Witch 1 And the result is … a classic Danish trophy.

Polonius I am told this is an item of great intrinsic value, constructed of multi-coloured gems from the future – though frankly if this is what gems will look like in the future I shall be glad to shuffle off this mortal coil before it happens.

Hamlet It will be curtains for you then.

Polonius Not sure what you are alluding to young man.

Ophelia Ignore him daddy. He is getting too Bardic for his own good.

Polonius And I present this magnificent trophy to—

There is a scuffle as all the Scots make a grab for it, and the Danes can't resist getting involved too. The cup is smashed in the mêlée!

Beth What's done is done.

Polonius So now – can we please all go home?

Macbeth This was a tale told by an idiot, full of sound and fury, signifying nothing.

Hamlet The rest is silence.

*** END OF MacHAMLET ***

Hamlet the Dane in Headley

Bard Again!

MacHamlet takes to foreign parts

Part 2 of the MacHamlet trilogy

Bard Again!

Cast List

The Scottish Team:

Mac Macbeth .... opportunist goal-seeker

Beth Macbeth .... his wife, team director

Witch One (Morag) .... organiser of Scottish cheerleaders

Witch Two (Kirsty) .... a cheery cheerleader

Witch Three (Bella) .... a dour cheerleader

Duncan King .... team captain

Banquo the Ghost .... a phantom winger

Birnam Wood .... from where we get defence

Glen & Morangie .... supporters of the Scottish distilleries

Will McGonagall [can double] .... a barred bard

The Danish Team:

Hamlet .... formerly known as Prince, dead ball specialist

Gertrude ... Hamlet's mother, team trainer, now married to Claudius

Claudius .... disputed team captain

Horatio .... a solid goalkeeper

Yorick .... good with the head

Polonius .... team manager

Ophelia .... team masseuse

Carl & Berg .... probably the best lager louts in the world

Hans Christian Andersen [can double] .... a seller of tales

Lady Godiva/Portia .... local referees

Kismet Kate .... an Italian feminist

Plus cameo roles which can all be doubled

The year is 1042; the time is medieval; the morals mighty evil!

List of Scenes

Act I

Scene 1   The Witches convene *(Front of Tabs)*

2   In a Scottish pub *(Full Set)*

3   Bard-off #1 *(Front of Tabs)*

4   Rowing practice *(Half Set)*

5   Witches' search *(Front of Tabs)*

6   On the Longboat *(Auditorium)*

7   The Venetians await *(Front of Tabs)*

8   Arrival in Venice *(Full Set)*

****   INTERVAL   ****

Act II

Scene 1   Polonius & Portia *(Front of Tabs)*

2   In a Venetian bar *(Full Set)*

3   Bard-off #2 *(Front of Tabs)*

4   Update (Front of Tabs)

5   Match of the Bay *(Full Set and in auditorium)*

6   Witches switch *(Front of tabs)*

7   Back in the Venetian bar *(Full Set)*

Glen & Morangie learn how to row

Bard Again!

<u>**Act I Scene 1**</u> **The Witches convene** *(Front of Tabs)*

(The three witches declaim from different points in the auditorium, moving towards the stage.)

Witch 1 The year has turned, the day is nigh.

Witch 2 'Once more unto the breach,' they cry.

Witch 3 'Once more unto the breach?' What's that?

Witch 1 We're off to see a football match

Witch 2 But not in Scotland, dear me no –
We've many further miles to go.

Witch 1 We'll have to go across the sea,
As far away as Italy.

Witch 3 To Italy? Well, thank you, ta –
I don't know if I go that far.

Witch 1 Well, Bella dear, that's nothing new.

Witch 2 It's true – she hasn't got a clue.

Witch 1 We're going there to cheer our lads.

Witch 2 Dressed in our tartan and our plaids.

Witch 3 Well count me out, it's not my scene.

Witch 1 Och, come on Bella, don't be mean!

Witch 2 They'll lose if we don't back them up.

Witch 3 Lose what?

Witch 1   The European Cup!

Witch 3 The wha'?

Witch 2   It's new this year you know.

Witch 1 The flying Doctor told us so.

Witch 3 Not that one in the flashing hut!

Witch 1 Aye, him again.

Witch 3   I don't know – but …

(They have arrived at the stage, and broomsticks appear)

Witch 2 You'll do it, Bella. Stick by me.
We'll travel in formation – see?

Witch 1 The Doctor found these on a trip.
He said we'd find them useful.

Witch 2   Sit
Like this, he said *(she demonstrates)* and hold on tight.

Witch 1 We'll be like three black crows in flight.

Witch 3 Where did he find them?

Witch 1   I don't know.
I think he said some studio.

Witch 2 Aye, piled outside with all the scrap
Along with some old wizard's hat.

Witch 3 They've all got names.

Witch 1   My, my, that's true.
I'm Harry Potter. Who are you?

Witch 2 I'm Weasley Ron.

Witch 3   I'm Hermi One.

Witch 1 Right – ready for a trial run?

Witch 2 As ready as we'll ever be.

Witch 1 Then, chocks away – to Italy!

(The witches exit, fly them if you dare!)

Act I Scene 2 **In a Scottish pub** *(Full Set)*

The pub is populated with Scottish revellers. There is a Lego trophy [see 'MacHamlet'] displayed in pride of place behind the bar.

Glen Have ye made it up with your wife yet Mac?

Macbeth Made it up? Made what up?

Morangie Disobeying manager's orders in the last football match. Is that what ye're referring to Glen?

Glen Aye, Morangie, that it is. She asked you specifically to take Duncan out, Mac.

Morangie And ye no' did do it.

Glen He was still on the pitch at the end of the game.

Morangie She was looking daggers at you, Mac.

Glen And ye know she's a dangerous woman where daggers are involved.

Macbeth Take out Duncan. How could I? The ref was on top of me all through the match.

Morangie Oh aye, maybe that's why the wife was looking daggers at you.

Glen Of course, considering who was doing the reffing.

Morangie That young lady from Coventry, Lady Godiva.

Glen With the FIFA card – whatever that is.

Macbeth Lady Godiva. She reffed our first match against the Danes, remember? When we won the trophy.

Morangie Aye, the Danish trophy. And we've won nothing since.

Macbeth Well anyway I didn't choose the ref. My wife did.

Glen As a lucky mascot?

Macbeth If so, it didn't work. We lost again. I think we should give up this football idea and go back to settling disputes with good old-fashioned rape and pillage.

Morangie Aye, I'm with you there Mac.

Glen Rape and pillage does it for me every time!

(Duncan, Banquo and Birnam Wood enter SR)

Duncan Wha's all this about rape and pillage?

Banquo Have we missed out on something?

Macbeth On your way, Dunc. I've trouble enough without you here.

Duncan Trouble wi' your rape and pillage, eh? Sounds like you need help!

Birnam We're pillage experts. Been taking them for years.

Macbeth *(To Duncan)* On your way, I said. The wife's on your case.

Duncan Oh, having the little woman sort out yer problems now, are you

Mac? Wha' d'ye keep in yer sporran?

Macbeth *(Rising)* Right, outside!

Duncan Delighted.

(Beth and Godiva enter SL)

Beth Are you boys at it again? No wonder this poor girl needs a drink.

Godiva No really, thanks – very kind of you and all that, but I'll just fill my water bladder and get on my horse back to Coventry.

Beth Lady, ye'll no refuse our hospitality. Give the girl a dram.

Macbeth Our hospitality is infamous. You wake up in the morning dead. Don't you Duncan?

Godiva Gosh, as tired as that? *(Takes the proffered glass)*

Macbeth No, I mean really dead. As in, lifeless.

Godiva I see.

Duncan Are you threatening me again, Macbeth!

(Blackout and sounds of thunder)

Beth See what happens when you make false accusations? Can we have our lights back again please.

(Lights return)

Beth Thank you kindly. You're welcome in our house any night Duncan. You know that.

Macbeth Aye, but ye'll leave in a box.

Banquo And you don't mean a penalty box.

(Macbeth and Duncan square up to each other)

Godiva *(Weaving between them)* Gosh, that was a strong dram. One of you may have to saddle my horse for me.

Macbeth I'll do that!

Duncan *(Speaking over Macbeth)* That'll be me!

Beth I think that will be my job, thank you boys.

Godiva Smashing. I'll be on my way then. Is my bladder full?

Macbeth On a wee dram? I doubt that. But you know where the midden is if you need it.

Beth *(Taking a full water bladder from Glen and handing it to Godiva)* This will be what she means. Come along, my Lady. I'll see you on your way.

Macbeth *(Looking at Godiva's attire)* You'll be wearing more than that riding through the Trossachs, won't you?

Godiva Golly yes. I've got a habit somewhere.

Duncan Is that like a riding cape?

Godiva A bit. I used to wear one of those – then I got out of the habit in Coventry.

Beth Time we left! *(She guides Godiva to the exit SR)*

Macbeth Will we see you again?

Godiva Depends on FIFA.

Beth They've seen quite enough already. Come on. *(They exit)*

Duncan Well that's it. Yer wife's seen the ref off, so we might as well head for the hills and get back to some good old-fashioned clan warfare.

Glen S'cot to be a good idea.

Birnam Then we'll take the high road...

Morangie ... And we'll take the low road.

Macbeth And the last man to fall is a Sassenach.

Banquo You'll not stand a ghost of a chance.

Glen Says who?

Morangie Yes, says who?

Birnam Says me and he, eh Banquo?

Banquo Aye, says we Birnam!

(There are the makings of a scuffle, when Beth re-enters)

Beth Boys, boys. Behave yourselves now. If it's a real scuffle you're after, look to the door.

Macbeth You're not turning us out now, are ye Beth?

Duncan *(To Macbeth)* Not before I've put an end to yer wailing.

Beth Boys, boys. Behind you! It's the beer-swilling huns.

(Hamlet enters SR to 'Air on a G string' smoking a small cigar)

(The stage manager enters quickly and takes the cigar from Hamlet.)

Stage Manager Sorry, no smoking in medieval times, remember?

(The music stops)

Hamlet We are back.

Beth So I observe. Danes. Back to raping and pillaging.

Macbeth Raping and pillaging still are ye? Heathens!

Duncan Have ye no' been civilised yet? Like us.

Beth Pardon me, it was imminent clan warfare two minutes ago.

Birnam They're bad losers.

Banquo One defeat at footba' and they're scared of another.

Glen Hung up yer boots, have ye?

Morangie Afraid of another drubbing?

(Enter SR Claudius, Horatio & Yorick, all with swords drawn)

Claudius We fear no man. We are sea wolves.

Macbeth Ye'll fear the missus then – she's a she wolf!

Hamlet Last time we were here she fed me poison.

Glen Poison? That was a 30-year-old single malt!

Macbeth Last time you were here you spiked our drinks with – wha' was it you called it?

Claudius Lager. Probably the best drink in the world.

Morangie <u>Your</u> world, maybe. Did you leave it at home this time?

(Enter SR Carl & Berg struggling with a crate or two of Carlsberg)

Obviously not!

Macbeth How <u>do</u> you drink that stuff?

Carl Straight from the bottle.

Beth Gnats could make better.

Hamlet We are here on a mission.

Duncan Not to spread that apology for a drink round the rest of the world I hope.

Berg We have been summoned.

Glen Summonsed? Under the influence of that?

Claudius He said summoned.

Glen Thank you officer, I'll remember that.

Claudius You mock the king of Denmark?

Hamlet He should not be king. He killed my dad. My dad should be king.

Duncan *(Ignoring Hamlet)* Ah yes, I remember ye now. Claudius. You and your wife.

Claudius And you are?

Duncan Duncan King. King of Scotland, remember?

Macbeth *Temporarily* King of Scotland. Until nightfall.

Beth I'll drink to that.

Claudius *(Ignoring the Macbeths)* And captain of the winning team when last we met – at football. I remember.

Duncan Aye.

Claudius You did not allow us to leave until we had provided a trophy.

Duncan Aye. It's still above the bar, look.

Beth When the kids aren't playing with it.

Claudius We have come to win the trophy back.

Duncan You want another game of football?

Claudius Not just one game, Mr King – a whole tournament of games.

(Enter SR Polonius & Ophelia)

Polonius Are you explaining the plan, Claudius?

Ophelia Hammie will explain it, won't you Hammie.

Hamlet Do not call me Hammie!

Ophelia Don't get touchy, Hammie.

Hamlet I'm not touchy, Feely!

Glen Touchy-feely sounds good to me, eh Morangie?

Morangie With you there, Glen.

Polonius My daughter is not Feely. She is Ophelia. Pray call her by her proper name or not at all.

Ophelia Get with it dad – no-one is going to call me Notta Tall.

Polonius Are you confusing me on purpose, daughter? Not difficult at my age, sadly.

Duncan Is one of you dithering Danes going to tell us what the Scott's going on?

(Gertrude enters SR)

Gertrude It is really very simple.

Duncan Well thank heaven for that!

Gertrude Football has gone global.

Macbeth You mean that game we played the other year instead of hacking each other's heads off?

Polonius You may not have heard, being across the water –

Banquo We're not across the water.

Birnam It's you that's across the water.

Polonius – but there is now a 'European Super League' as I believe it is called.

Duncan 'European'! Are we European?

Polonius Technically, yes.

Duncan Well slap me sporran!

Polonius I think I shall ignore that invitation.

Macbeth So who else is in this 'European Super League'?

Polonius Well we are.

Duncan Obviously, or you wouldn't be coming here to hassle us.

Hamlet The usual suspects. Germany, France, Poland...

Polonius Does Poland exist at the moment?

Hamlet Yes – it tends to come and go, but at the moment...

Macbeth The English? Are they in it?

Polonius You mean the lady from Coventry?

Beth We've only just got rid of her.

Hamlet They have a new king, Edward the Confessor. He seems more interested in building cathedrals than playing football.

Polonius I believe the Normans are fielding a team.

Duncan If they don't beat the English, we will.

Beth And where is the action to happen?

Polonius In Venice.

Glen Venice? Isn't that the place with the flooded streets?

Polonius I believe it is.

Morangie And the little black boats...

Glen ...Wi' a wee singer standing at the back.

Polonius That will be a future affectation, or so I am told.

Macbeth How do they fit a football pitch in a flooded city?

Polonius We shall find out when we get there.

Duncan Get there? How are we getting there?

Macbeth Have you been talking to that Doctor fellow again?

Polonius Who?

Macbeth Aye, that's the one. The one with the flying cupboard.

Hamlet We need no flying cupboards. We have boats.

Horatio Long boats...

Yorick ...which go long distances.

Beth That gets you there. What about us?

Polonius We are here to offer you transport.

Morangie In one of those open boats...?

Glen ...Wi' a row of rowers?

Morangie I feel seasick already!

Glen We'll need a few steadying drams, Morangie.

Gertrude You will not feel sick when you are rowing.

Banquo Rowing?

Birnam Us?

Duncan I get the idea. Ye tire us out so we're in no fit state to play when we get there.

Macbeth I think I'll opt for the flying cupboard.

Gertrude We shall all be rowing.

Beth All of us?

Macbeth My wife's not fit to row.

Beth And you think that you are?

Gertrude You will all be fit by the time we leave. I am arranging for some practice to happen.

Duncan Every time you Danes turn up we have to get fit. I wish you'd stay at home.

Gertrude We are rovers by nature.

Macbeth Like Raith, you mean.

Duncan Shouldn't be difficult to beat then.

Claudius Sea wolves.

Banquo Wolves?

Birnam They're a rubbish team too.

Gertrude Enough of this. Carl and Berg will be in charge of training.

Horatio Possibly the best pair of trainers in the world.

Beth We'll have Glen and Morangie help them.

Banquo They've got a lot of bottle.

Gertrude Then see to your to rowlocks everyone!

Claudius My oars, my oars – a kingdom for my oars!

Macbeth *(To Beth)* Are you sure this is a good idea?

Beth We'll no' know till we try it – come on.

(Curtain closes as they exit)

<u>Act I Scene 3</u> **Bard-off #1** *(Front of Tabs)*

(The bards enter from opposite sides)

Hans Christian Andersen Here we are again, William.

Will McGonagall Filling in between the scenes, Hans.

Hans Odious!

Will Barbaric.

Hans More matter with less art.

Will Out, out, brief candle!

Hans Now just a minute. We should not be thinking of home.

Will Wha' d'you mean?

Hans Those quotes we were about to quote.

Will Fine quotes from the Scottish Play!

Hans And there is nothing rotten in the state of Denmark either, but we must think ahead. We must think of our destination, of Italy.

Will Are there bardic quotes from Italy?

Hans There were Two Gentlemen of Verona.

Will Aye, but with only two quotable quotes between them.

Hans Which are?

Will A man I am, crossed with adversity.

Hans I am sorry to hear that, Will – but what were the quotes?

Will That was one of the quotes. Is she not passing fair?

Hans Fair to middling, Will – but what is the other?

Will That was the other.

Hans Oh, I am sorry. I had not realised. Perhaps we should try the Merchant of Venice.

Will Aye. In the twinkling of an eye.

Hans If you prick us, do we not bleed?

Will My own flesh and blood.

Hans Thy pound of flesh.

Will My ventures are not in one bottom trusted.

Hans It is a wise father that knows his own child.

Will I dote on his very absence.

Hans All that glisters is not gold.

Will The quality of mercy is not strained.

Hans There is no power in the decrees of Venice.

Will It droppeth as the gentle rain from heaven.

Hans Give me your hand, McGonagall; fare you well.

(They shake hands & exit on opposite sides)

First Interval if you are serving a 2-course meal to the audience

<u>**Act I Scene 4**</u> **Rowing practice** *(Half Set)*

(The stage is set up for rowing practice – Carl & Berg enter with an oar)

Carl So we are to teach the Scotch to row.

Berg That is the task we have been given.

Carl What have we done to deserve this?

Berg We were probably standing in the wrong place at the wrong time.

Carl That is true. Here come our first pupils – *(Glen & Morangie enter)* – and they do not look very promising.

Glen Are you the pair of lager louts who's going tae teach us rowing?

Berg We are a pair, we drink lager and we are going to teach you rowing, yes.

Carl But I do not know if we are louts. You will tell us if we are louts?

Glen Oh aye, we'll tell you, lout and clear!

Morangie *(Looking at the oar)* Is this the paddle we use?

Carl Yes, that is the paddle we use.

Berg We call it 'an oar'.

Glen An or what?

Berg Just an oar. An oar is an oar.

Carl You do not know about oars?

72

Morangie Aye, ye get them walking down Sauchiehall Street in Glasgow on a Saturday night.

Carl Pardon?

Glen How do you use your oars?

Berg We lash them to the side of the boat and pull their handles.

Morangie Their handles?

Carl It is not difficult. We will show you.

Berg And you will soon get used to travelling backwards. We do it all the time.

Glen I'm surprised you ever get to where you're going.

Carl Sometimes that is a problem – particularly in the fog.

Berg Then we put a man up the mast.

Glen Does that help?

Berg No, but there is always someone who has been naughty, and it is a good place to put him. Out of sight, out of mind.

Carl *(Indicating a rowing machine)* Here is your seat. Sit down please.

Morangie Where in the eleventh century did you get this?

Carl We raided *[local sports centre]*.

Berg Told *[the receptionist]* it was rag week.

Carl *(Indicating his helmet)* You can get away with it when your helmets have big horns. Now, are you sitting comfortably?

        (Glen & Morangie are each sitting in a rowing machine)

Glen Aye, but I don't have a helmet with a big horn.

Carl Now we shall set your dial to – let me think – from here to Venice – ja, 4,000 miles will be about right.

Morangie Four thousand miles?

Carl We may stop off at Gibraltar for a rest half way, but you should train for the full 4,000 just in case.

Morangie *(Again)* Four thousand miles? How long will that take?

Berg On the sea – about three weeks.

Carl But on this machine you can knock them off in a few days, no problem.

Glen A few days? We're supposed to sit here on this contraption for a few days?

Morangie How boring is that?

Carl No, no – you do not just sit on it – you work it. Like this.

(He demonstrates using the machine)

And the harder you pull, the faster you go. In, out, two out …

Berg And you see here the picture of your movement through the water. Cute, eh?

Glen The picture is all blue.

Berg The water is all blue. What do you expect?

Morangie Not much in the way of scenery then.

Glen Watching a blue screen for hours on end.

Morangie *(To Glen)* What was it the Doctor said about watching a blue screen?

Glen "Bloody Microsoft!" I think it was.

Carl Well, if you are both settled in …

Berg … we will leave you to it for an hour or two and go and see to the others.

Both Farvel!

(Carl & Berg exit)

Glen And 'farvel' to you too.

Morangie Come on Glen, only another 3,999 miles to go. You can do it. I'll race you to the next wave top.

Glen Go wet yerself!

Morangie Please yerself. I'll get to Venice afore you. Last one there's …

Glen A Sassenach Dane!

(The curtains close on them as they continue rowing)

Act I Scene 5 Witches' search *(Front of Tabs)*

(Witches enter SL)

Witch 3 Are we there yet?

Witch 1 <u>We</u> are.

Witch 2 <u>They're</u> not.

Witch 3 Who's not?

Witch 1 The motley crew's not.

Witch 2 The tartan army.

Witch 1 The flower of Scotland.

Witch 3 Where are they then?

Witch 2 Good question. Do we have them on witch watch Morag?

Witch 1 *(Getting out mobile phone)* I keep trying this thing but it always says 'no signal'. It worked alright when we were with the Doctor.

Witch 2 He did say reception was a bit poor in medieval times.

Witch 3 Are we in medieval times?

Witch 1 *(Looking at the audience)* This lot look like the Doctor's friends. *(To audience)* Are we in medieval times?

Witch 2 I think someone said very evil times.

Witch 1 *(To audience)* Will our witch watch work here? *(To Witch 2)* They say not if it's *[whatever system gives bad reception locally]*.

Witch 2 Perhaps you have to shout, like the Doctor says you do when you're on a train.

Witch 1 *(Shouting into phone)* 'Allo, 'allo. 'Allo, 'allo.

*

Witch 1 No luck.

Witch 2 Not sure, but I think you may have woken somebody.

Witch 3 By the pricking of my thumbs,
    Maybe a technician comes.

---

* In the original script, here the Witches met a succession of characters from plays which the company had performed recently.

(Kate enters SL)

Witch 3 Are you a technician?

Kate Do you mean a Mechanical?

Witch 2 A mechanical what?

Kate Mr Shakespeare likes mechanicals.

Witch 1 I'm sure he does, but do they fix phones?

Kate If you ask me to make a shrewd guess, I'd say no.

Witch 2 A shrewd guess. Is that a clue to your character?

Kate Indeed – I am the shrewd Shrew. Kate the Shrew, to be tamed on Mr Shakespeare's instructions.

Witch 3 That Mr Shakespeare! He sets this whole play going and then disappears.

Kate Like a phantom into the night.

Witches Wrong play!

Kate But a shrewd move. If I could get my hands on Mr misogynist Shakespeare I'd tell him a thing or two.

Witch 2 Such as?

Kate Such as, getting him to change that speech he forces me to say at the end of the play. What do you think of: "Place your hands below your husband's foot" and "If he please, My hand is ready, may it do him ease."

Witch 3 Sounds like he's in trouble if you find him.

Kate Believe me, that's just the start of it. *(Exits SR)*

Witch 1 If I see him I'll warn him. Tsch! This wretched phone still isn't working!

(A stage hand appears briefly)

Stage Hand Here borrow mine – it gets a signal here.

Witch 1 Oh, cheers. *(Reacts as he disappears again)* Who was that?

Witch 2 A handy man.

Witch 3 Is it working?

Witch 1 Seems to be. Now, what's their number?

Witch 2 It'll probably be under 'Mac Mob'.

Witch 3 I don't know how you hit the right buttons with finger nails like yours.

(Witches exit SL still debating the number to ring)

<u>Act I Scene 6</u> **On the Longboat** *(Auditorium)*

(The cast appear rowing through the auditorium)

Gertrude In – out – two – out – three – out …

Macbeth All out! Rest your oars, you Scots. We're doing no more.

Gertrude If you Scots stop now, the boat will go round in circles.

Macbeth Then you shouldn't have put us all on one side.

Beth Mac, you're letting the side down.

Macbeth We're not made for this. Let's see them toss a caber.

Duncan Aye, let's see what sort of tossers they are.

Claudius This will not get us to Venice.

Macbeth D'you not have a sail to put up on yon mast?

Gertrude To use a sail you need the wind.

Duncan Are you getting personal now?

Banquo We've not been getting our porridge.

Birnam Aye, we can't row boats without our oats.

Horatio You were offered a Danish pastry for breakfast. But you refused.

Banquo We've been travelling for a week now. They're not exactly fresh.

Yorick We are happy to eat them.

Birnam You may be, but even the seagulls refused to eat mine.

(There is the sound of a mobile phone ringing)

Macbeth *(To audience)* Oh dear. Who's forgotten to switch off their phone?

Duncan There's always one.

Macbeth Come on – who is it? Own up.

Beth I think it's yours, Mac.

Macbeth Mine?

Beth Aye – in your sporran.

Macbeth *(Getting his phone out)* Oh – I forgot. The witches' curse. You will never have another peaceful moment in your life. Hello? Oh, hi Morag – yes – how're you doing? No – we're ON THE BOAT – Yes – Yes – Well no, not right now I can't – Because I'm supposed to be rowing a boat. We're just passing Gibraltar. Alright. Yes. See you in a few days – And you. Bye. *(He puts the phone away)*

Beth What's this "and you"?

Macbeth She was wishing me well.

Beth She's a witch – witches don't wish anybody well, least of all you.

Claudius What is going on over there? Why have you stopped?

Gertrude They have no spirit.

Glen Spirit – did someone mention spirit, Morangie?

Morangie That's what I heard, Glen.

Beth Don't start that again. You'll get them all intoxicated if you mention spirit on this side of the boat.

Hamlet We are wasting good weather. Let us row on.

Beth It's alright. My husband became a little bewitched, but it will pass.

(They start to row again)

Hamlet That is better. Feely is making good strokes over here.

Polonius She would do better if she kept her hands on the oars.

Hamlet She is the team masseuse is she not?

Polonius She is also my daughter, and the strokes she is making are not appropriate.

Ophelia Hammie was a little stiff. It is not comfortable to be stiff when you are rowing.

Horatio How would you know that, Feely?

Yorick Imagination, Horatio – there are more things in heaven and earth…

Carl Are you coming down the line, Feely?

Berg There are a few of us stiffening up along here.

Duncan Hey, and what about us Scots? We don't have a masseuse.

Macbeth We have my wife, Dunc. She'll give you a good going over.

Banquo Aye, With a dagger.

Beth Will you boys stop your squabbling and pull?

Gertrude Well said. Let us see Sicily by sunset.

Claudius And Malta by moonlight.

Hamlet And Venice by Vednesday.

Macbeth It's all getting very romantic over that side.

Beth Just dig your oars in Mac and think of Scotland.

Macbeth That sounds very familiar!

(They exit 'rowing' through side doors by the stage)

<u>**Act I Scene 7**</u> **The Venetians Await** *(Half Set)*

(Kate enters SR)

Kate Old fashions please me best; I am not so nice
To change true rules for odd inventions.

(Portia enters SL – she was Godiva in Scene 1)

Portia There is no power in the decrees of Venice.

Kate Sorry. And you are…?

Portia Portia. Like the car.

Kate Pardon? Car?

Portia Golly, no you won't have met the Doctor will you. Brings news from the future. Horseless carriages and all that. One of them will be named after me he says – Porsche.

Kate Do you belong here?

Portia Not in Scene 1 I didn't – but I do now, I think. I'm supposed to be one of Mr Shakespeare's Italian creations.

Kate Supposed to be?

Portia The four winds blow in from every coast renownèd suitors,

and my sunny locks hang on my temples like a golden fleece.
Like it?

Kate Not a lot.

Portia Well that's Mr Shakespeare for you. Who are you?

Kate I am called plain Kate. A household Kate.

Portia By Mr Shakespeare? Golly – I think I got the better part then.

Kate What is your part?

Portia Mr Shakespeare had me down as a rich heiress who knows a thing or two about the Quality of Mercy.

Kate What do you know about it?

Portia It is not strained.

Kate Is that all?

Portia Pretty much, yes. But it got me this job with FIFA.

Kate FIFA. Is that another car?

Portia Golly no. You're thinking of Fiat. FIFA's to do with football.

Kate Football.

Portia I'm reffing the competition here.

Kate Reffing. Football. I do not find these words in Mr Shakespeare's texts.

Portia Football wasn't big in Mr Shakespeare's day.

Kate Can you describe this football to me?

Portia I think it's probably indescribable.

Kate Beyond description?

Portia You have to be in it to win it.

Kate I am intrigued – tell me more.

Portia Best be in Venice on Sunday and you'll see us in action.

Kate I will to Venice; Sunday comes apace.

Portia In the twinkling of an eye.

(They exit the way they came)

<u>Act I Scene 8</u> **Arrival in Venice** *(Full Set)*

      (The longboat has arrived – the Scots stagger ashore)

Macbeth Rowlocks!

Beth Language, Mac!

Macbeth I never want to see another rowlock again.

Glen I've got blisters all over.

Morangie All over what, Glen?

Glen All over everywhere.

Birnam I've got blisters on my blisters.

Banquo I'm not saying what I've got blisters on.

Duncan We're in no state to play football, that's certain.

Beth What's happened to my hardy clansmen? You're out in all weathers on the moors wearing skirts wi' no knickers, and look at ye now.

Macbeth No knickers! That was the problem.

Glen Rough wooden seats, wi' no knickers.

Morangie I'll bet the Danes had their knickers on.

Beth Well, d'you know, I never asked.

Duncan Here's your chance.

      (The Danes enter looking fit)

Birnam *(Looking at the Danes)* Not a blister in sight.

Banquo I think we were talking about blisters that were out of sight.

Gertrude Nothing is better than a sea voyage to get you fit for action.

Glen Aye, I'll drink to that.

Morangie Nothing is <u>far</u> better than a sea voyage.

Claudius Do you not feel your muscles are now well toned?

Macbeth Some of my muscles have got no feeling at all.

Birnam I've a feeling I'd rather be standing than sitting for a good wee while.

Horatio Perhaps you were not wearing the padded pants.

Yorick   Every Dane wears the padded pants. From an early age.

Duncan   Padded pants? It's not manly!

Hamlet   We only wear them when we are rowing.

Ophelia   Saves you from bruising your bits, doesn't it Hammie.

Hamlet   At other times we wear…

Ophelia   This could be interesting. Go on, Hammie.

Hamlet   …conventional underwear.

Duncan   Ye'll no' catch Scots wearing conventional underwear. We brave the moors unfettered.

Ophelia   Do you hear that, Hammie? Unfettered. We could start a whole new unfettered fashion in Elsinore.

Hamlet   We have stone seats in Elsinore, Feely. Cold stone seats. I do not think it would catch on.

Ophelia   Oh well, stick to your 'conventional underwear' then.

Hamlet   I do – often.

Polonius   Ahem! I think we have all heard quite enough about underwear now, thank you.

Gertrude   More to the point, where is our football to be played? Where is the welcoming committee.

Beth   A welcoming committee for Danes? That's a novelty!

Macbeth   They're probably hiding their women and children right now.

Polonius   I was under the impression that we were invited here.

Duncan   Just because you're invited doesn't mean you're welcome. Ask your man here. *(Points to Macbeth)*

Beth   You've always been welcome in our house Duncan. What makes you think you're not.

Duncan   The dagger that you hide about your person, woman, that's what.

Gertrude   *(To Beth)* Daggers are so last century, dear. Poison is the thing to use these days. Isn't that so Claudius?

Hamlet   You admit it! You poisoned my father! You poured poison in his ears.

Ophelia Calm down, Hammie dear.

Polonius I do rather think that we have a certain amount of pre-match tension building up here. Not good for team spirit.

Glen Team spirit!

Morangie That's what we're missing, Glen! Where is it?

Glen I thought you were bringing it, Morangie.

Morangie And I thought you were.

Hamlet Are you talking of that spirit you nearly killed me with last time?

Glen We're talking of the single malt.

Morangie A concoction distilled in heaven. Or in the Scottish highlands, which is much the same thing.

Glen It's back on the boat.

Morangie Then we'd best go and get it before the locals do. *(They exit)*

Macbeth *(To Hamlet)* It'll be fighting spirit when we get it inside us.

Hamlet We Danes have our own way of refreshing ourselves.

Beth Not wi' that gnat's water of yours!

Polonius We are told that it is probably …

Beth …the best drink in the world. Aye, we heard.

Gertrude Carl and Berg are in charge of it. Perhaps you would like a crate as a gift. *(Carl & Berg exit)*

Duncan Don't touch the stuff. It's like lead in your stomach. You'll not last the 90 minutes with tha' inside you.

Hamlet But it does not blow your head off like the whisky does.

Duncan It only blows the heads off disbelievers. And lager drinkers.

(Glen & Morangie return with a crate of whisky)

Beth Well here's your chance to join us in a dram.

Macbeth You're privileged. She doesn't offer it to just anyone, you know.

Gertrude A bottle in one hand and a dagger in the other, or so I have heard.

Beth That's rich coming from a poisoner's wife.

Polonius May I bring this meeting to order?

Ophelia Would that be order for a lager or a whisky?

Polonius You are not helping, daughter. I am attempting to smooth the water.

(Carl & Berg return with a crate of Carlsberg)

Duncan And talking of water, here it comes.

Polonius We could, I suppose, mix the two together. How would that be?

Scots & Danes *(in unison)* Sacrilege!

Polonius Ah well, one can but try. Blessèd are the peacemakers.

Macbeth We don't need a blessèd peacemaker.

Hamlet We need a blessèd drink!

Macbeth Let's get stuck in lads!

(The crates are opened and the contents also)

Gertrude Should you not be having some food with that?

Duncan Aye, a wee snack wouldn't go amiss. What are you offering lass?

Gertrude What would you say to *(what the audience will get during the interval)*.

Macbeth That will do us nicely.

Gertrude No, that is what the audience is getting. For you we have Danish pastries and bacon.

Beth And as a Scots treat I've brought some oats from home. We can make a nice cauldron of porridge.

Hamlet I hope that is not all that you have brought from home.

Macbeth You want some haggis?

Hamlet I do not know – what is this haggis?

Beth A sheep's stomach, filled with...

Gertrude ...filled with its entrails. Or that is what I am told by those who have survived eating it.

Ophelia It is no wonder that they wear no underwear then, eh Hammie?

Hamlet It is not what I meant when I asked what else you had brought from home. I was not thinking of food.

Gertrude You call that haggis food?

Hamlet I was thinking of the trophy.

Macbeth The trophy is safe.

Hamlet I am glad to hear that. Where is it?

Macbeth Safe in my sporran.

Hamlet Where?

Macbeth Here *(slaps his sporran)* in my sporran. Oh dear!

Ophelia I think that may have been a slap too hard.

> *(Macbeth puts his hand in his sporran and brings out*
> *a handful of multicoloured bricks)*

Macbeth *(repeats)* Oh dear!

Beth So much for Danish products. One tiny tap and they're in pieces.

Gertrude They are not meant to be slapped by hairy-handed Scotsmen.

Beth I know what you mean, dear. None of us like to be slapped by hairy-handed Scotsmen.

Ophelia Oh, I don't know though.

Polonius Daughter, that is enough. This is a serious matter.

Hamlet If she likes being slapped by hairy-handed Scotsmen, it is a very serious matter.

Polonius We must have the trophy reinstated.

Beth How can we make a trophy out of that pile of bricks?

> *(Business with the audience)*

Banquo Ask some children to do it?

Birnam Do we have any children here?

Banquo I think we may have to make do with who we've got.

Macbeth Who!

All WHAT?

Macbeth The doctor wi' the flying cupboard. He can do it.

Gertrude And where is he?

Macbeth *(Bringing his mobile out of his sporran)* I don't know, but I know a hag who does. *(Keys in a number)* Hello Morag. We have a wee problem here.

Beth I'll gi' you a wee problem if you keep phoning that hag. What's she got that I haven't got?

Duncan What's she got that you haven't got? Where shall we start, Beth.

Beth That's enough from you, Duncan King, or it'll be daggers before dawn.

Macbeth *(Still on his phone)* Aye, if you could, that would be great. Be seeing you then. And you. Bye. *(Closes his phone)* Sorted!

Beth And what's fancy drawers doing for you now, then?

Macbeth You'll see.

Beth Oh I'll see, will I? Well not before you've seen...

        (The three Witches arrive, each carrying a bag of Lego)

Witch 1 Morag!

Witch 2 Kirsty!

Witch 3 Bella!

All Witches Back on cue.

Witch 1 With greetings from the Doctor...

Witch 2 Who...

Witch 3 ...has given us...

Witch 1 ...not one...

Witch 2 ...not two...

Witch 3 ...but three Lego trophy repair kits.

Polonius And who will do this repair?

Witch 1 No, sadly he couldn't come himself. But he made a suggestion.

Witch 2 Give the kits out to the audience...

Witch 3 ...and the best trophy constructed by the end of the evening wins...

Polonius A trophy?

Witch 1 Who knows. We'll distribute these...

Witch 2 ...and you get on with the show.

(The Witches distribute the bags of Lego among the audience)

Polonius Ah yes, the show – we had rather forgotten there was a script to follow.

Macbeth Aye, sorry – that was my fault. Always been heavy-handed.

Hamlet No need to apologise. All's well that ends well.

Macbeth Ends well? That's neither my play nor yours then.

Hamlet No, you are right. They do not end well. Perhaps this one will be better.

(During this time the rest of the cast are getting bored & starting to exit)

Macbeth You think so?

Hamlet I do not know.

Macbeth It is a different author.

Hamlet And we are in Italy now. Perhaps that leads to happier results.

Macbeth Romeo & Juliet? I don't think so.

Hamlet The Taming of the Shrew?

Macbeth Aye, maybe. If you're not a woman.

Hamlet That is true.

Polonius *(Remaining on stage)* Pardon me for intruding…

Hamlet *(Still speaking to Macbeth)* You know, it's no fun having your name constantly associated with tragedy.

Macbeth Tell me about it! And in my case no-one will even speak my name.

Polonius Hello!

Hamlet At least they did not name a cigar after you.

Macbeth If they had it would have been an exploding cigar.

Polonius Can I just say…

Hamlet A cigar called Mac…

Macbeth Dinna say it laddie!

Polonius …that the First Act has finished, and we are about to serve food.

Macbeth Food? Och, sorry. *(To audience)* Sorry – we were reminiscing.

Hamlet Our two plays do not meet very often and it is a rare chance to catch up on things.

Macbeth Aye that's true. So, enjoy your food. We'll be having stale Danish pastries.

Hamlet But we will see you refreshed in the second half, ja?

Polonius Yes indeed. Thank you ladies and gentlemen. Food will be brought to you by Venetian valets. Do not forget to construct your colourful trophies. And *bon appetit* as I believe our French cousins will one day say.

(The curtain falls)

*** INTERVAL ***

Act II Scene 1 Polonius & Portia *(Front of Tabs)*

(Polonius enters SL)

Polonius Now I feel you may need a little guidance as to what is going on here. As do I. As far as I can see, the situation appears to be as follows…

(Portia enters SR)

Portia Excuse me.

Polonius My good lady, certainly I will excuse you. What for?

Portia Oh golly, I don't know. For interrupting you, I suppose.

Polonius My dear, interruptions from young ladies like yourself are always welcome – and sadly all too rare these days.

Portia I was looking for the football pitch.

Polonius Incredible – you must have read my ellipsis.

Portia *(Looking at his lips)* No, I don't think so. I heard you perfectly well.

Polonius My ellipsis, dear girl. The hanging end of my utterance.

Portia Where are you from?

Polonius We hail from Denmark. Elsinore to be precise.

Portia Golly – do you all speak like that there?

Polonius Like what where?

Portia Like telling me about the hanging end of your utterance.

Polonius I was merely trying to explain that in my opening peroration I was just about to say that we also are looking for the football pitch – when you entered and made my own nascent question redundant. My line ended in an ellipsis.

Portia Oh, that's a nasty way to go.

Polonius I beg your pardon?

Portia Your line, ending like that. Did they catch it from a parrot?

Polonius A parrot?

Portia This lipsis-thing. You catch it from parrots, don't you.

Polonius Young lady, are you thinking of psittacosis?

Portia Not often. Is that a big word for a pain in the bottom?

Polonius No, but I am close to applying it to you if it were.

Portia Golly, I'm well lost. Can we start again?

Polonius By all means. You were looking for a football pitch here in Venice – and as it happens, so was I.

Portia All the way from Denmark.

Polonius I cannot deny it.

Portia I've just popped down the Po from Parma. Name's Portia.

Polonius *(Shaking hands)* Polonius. Lord Chamberlain to the King of Denmark – and for my sins, manager of his football team.

Portia Ooo-er! In that case we'd better not fraternise – I'm one of the match referees.

Polonius A lady referee. Oh dear – I think I'm having one of my old fashioned feelings coming on.

Portia You don't approve of lady refs?

Polonius We had a lady referee when we lost to the Scots in our very first match.

Portia Was she fair?

Polonius Come to think of it, she looked a lot like you.

Portia Most refs look the same when they're stripped for action.

Polonius Stripped. Yes, well …

Portia But there'll be no action here unless we can find the football pitch.

Polonius Very true, and Venice is not best known for its verdant pastures.

Portia I was told to search for the island of Sant'Elena.

Polonius Who told you that?

Portia Yes. How did you guess?

Polonius How did I guess what?

Portia That Who told me.

Polonius Madam, you are losing me.

Portia Well, we can't have that. Let's look for it together.

Polonius If you insist. I think I am about to lose my objectivity.

Portia And at your age too!

(They exit together)

Act II Scene 2 In a Venetian bar *(Full Set)*

There is the sound of Italian music – Kate is behind the bar
(Glen, Morangie, Carl & Berg enter UR)

Glen This one will do, lads.

Carl It does not look very lively in here.

Morangie We'll soon change that!

Glen *(To Kate)* Are you open for business, lassie.

Kate They call me Katherine that do talk of me.

Carl The lady doth protest too much, methinks.

Morangie There's no art to find the mind's construction in the face.

Kate Am I to be surrounded by Mr Shakespeare's quotations.

Berg To be or not to be, that is the question. I will go tell the others. *(Exits)*

Glen Aye, get the teams in. We'll find what Katherine has hidden behind her bar.

Kate Katherine will keep her own company behind her bar, thank you.

Carl There is Italian hospitality for you!

Morangie After rowing for weeks. If I'd wanted a sour-faced barmaid I could have stayed at home.

Glen We've got plenty of those in Scotland.

Carl And in Elsinore they are not so wonderful. Maybe when we get Copenhagen it will be wonderful, but not yet.

Kate I assume you are the male chauvinist football supporters we were told to expect from abroad.

Glen Supporters? No, we're players.

Morangie Match fit and ready to go.

Kate Well, you can go as soon as you like. The bar is closed.

Carl Then what is the sign on the door? It says 'Aperto'.

Kate And soon it will say 'Chiuso'. I have a home to go to.

Glen Would that be a home for hard-hearted bar staff?

Morangie I hope they look after you well in it.

*(Suddenly the bar is filled by the return of Berg
with all the others except Polonius)*

Berg This is the place.

Macbeth D'you think they do a decent dram here?

Duncan I'd go for an indecent dram at the moment.

Beth You could do wi' some decent food in you first.

Gertrude Are you saying we did not feed you on the boat?

Birnam I think we've said that a number of times.

Banquo Have they invented pizza here yet?

Birnam Aye. Deep-fried pizza…

Banquo …Wi' chips.

Kate The bar is closed.

Macbeth Say that again?

Kate Closed. Chiuso. Lukket. Whatever language it is you speak.

Duncan See here lassie…

Glen No good Dunc, I've tried the buttering up. She's a hard case.

Morangie A hard-faced case.

Carl She appears not to like men.

Beth Well that's understandable.

Gertrude A woman with some sense.

Beth You men stand aside.

Gertrude Ophelia, disengage yourself from Hamlet and come over here.

Beth *(To Kate)* Have these men been giving you trouble?

Kate I can look after myself. Men do not trouble me.

Macbeth *(Calling)* She eats them for breakfast.

Gertrude Ignore the oafs. They are Scottish.

Kate We have similar in Italy, but here the oafs are better dressed.

Ophelia You will have to show us.

Kate I will not need to – they will find you.

Beth Aye, she's a fine piece of Danish on the hoof.

Gertrude Polonius will have his work cut out keeping an eye on her here.

Ophelia Do not, as some ungracious pastors do, show me the steep and thorny way to heaven.

Kate I like your quote, and your spirit.

Duncan *(Calling)* Did someone mention spirits again?

Beth Shut your mouth Duncan, we're having peace talks here.

Kate *(To Ophelia)* You surely are not part of a football team.

Gertrude She is the team masseuse. She refreshes the parts that other members cannot reach.

Ophelia Something like that. Yes.

Beth Or so Hamlet tells us.

Kate Hamlet? You have the eponymous Hamlet here? The great Dane?

Ophelia Oh, he's not always so great you know. Sometimes…

Gertrude Thank you Ophelia – I think we get the message.

Horatio I think he gets the message when he gets the massage!

Kate But he is one of Mr Shakespeare's greatest inventions.

Ophelia Do you hear that Hammie? – you're an invention.

Beth You study the Bard here?

Kate Mr Shakespeare has set many of his works in Italy. You say you are from Scotland?

Beth Aye.

Kate Then you must be…

Beth Don't say it lass, or you'll call down the powers of evil.

Kate … Lady Macbeth!

(Blackout and sounds of thunder)

Beth What did I tell you?

Hamlet Did somebody say that word?

Macbeth The curse follows us everywhere.

Duncan You deserve it for your black deeds.

Hamlet He is not the only one. What about Claudius the dirty Dane?

Gertrude Do not speak of your king in that way.

Hamlet He should not be king! He should be…

Beth Excuse me. Can we have our lights back again please.

(Lights return)

Thank you.

Kate So, you are here for the football.

Claudius We are here for revenge.

Gertrude The Scots beat us last time we met on the field.

Claudius It was not a field – it was a blasted heath. That is why we lost.

Duncan That's a poor excuse. Ye would have lost on any pitch.

Hamlet We do not know what sort of pitch it will be this time.

(Polonius and Portia enter UR)

Polonius Sadly, we <u>do</u> know what sort of pitch it will be.

Portia A very wet pitch.

Beth *(To Portia)* Don't I recognise you from Scene 1?

Portia *(Stage whisper)* I'm doubling. Lady Godiva and Portia.

Polonius Ahem. There were plans to build a fine stadium on an island specially constructed called Sant'Elena.

Portia But the plans got put back...

Polonius Budgetary constraints...

Portia And the stadium never materialised.

Polonius It is worse than that – the island never materialised.

Claudius So where are we playing this football?

Portia The rules have been slightly altered.

Polonius There will still be a ball and goals at each end...

Portia ...but you will be swimming between them. And you do not use your feet.

Polonius The locals inform me that this version of football is called water polo.

Portia Very popular in Venice.

Duncan And what if ye canna swim?

Polonius Visiting teams will be allowed to use inflatable aids.

Macbeth Inflatable aids? What's tha' when it's at home?

Polonius We have yet to find out.

Kate Well while you are waiting to find out, would anybody like a drink?

Glen We thought you'd never ask.

Morangie I thought you said you were closed.

Kate That was before I knew you were Mr Shakespeare's men. The Bard's men are never barred.

(Curtain)

94

<u>**Act II Scene 3**</u> **Bard-off #2** *(Front of Tabs)*

(The bards enter from opposite sides)

Will McGonagall Mr Andersen, I remember a previous time when we met and you gave that splendid rendition of the tale of the Ugly Duckling.

Hans Christian Andersen I remember it too, Mr McGonagall. And I also remember that your equally impressive rendition of some home-spun Scottish verse of yours was the winner in our competition that day. As judged by Mr Shakespeare.

Will Mr Shakespeare himself. No praise could be higher.

Hans No. Except that the judgement of history may remember the Ugly Duckling for longer than your verse, I think.

Will Do I detect the tone of a bad loser, Mr Andersen.

Hans You do not, Mr McGonagall. These one-off competitions have a habit of bringing strange offerings to the stage. I prefer the test of time.

Will Well, are ye up for another competition or noo?

Hans You have another offering?

Will I do – and about none other than the Bard himself.

Hans About the Bard. I cannot wait!

Will Immortal! William Shakespeare, there's none can you excel,
You have drawn out your characters remarkably well,
Which is delightful for to see enacted upon the stage
For instance, the love-sick Romeo, or Othello, in a rage;
His writings are a treasure, which the world cannot repay,
He was the greatest poet of the past or of the present day
Also the greatest dramatist, and is worthy of the name,
I'm afraid the world shall never look upon his like again.
His tragedy of Hamlet is moral and sublime,
And for purity of language, nothing can be more fine
For instance, to hear the fair Ophelia making her moan,
At her father's grave, sad and alone...

Hans Making Feely moan? Who did that?

Will No – "making her moan" is a poetic way of saying she was doing the moaning – she was 'making the moan'.

Hans Then why not say so?

Will   Sometimes I feel you cannot have a poetic bone in your body, Mr Andersen. It is the way we poets speak.

Hans   If you say so Mr McGonagall. Have you finished now?

Will   Not quite – but since you do not appreciate my style, I will cut to the end.

Hans   That is good.

Will   Immortal! Bard of Avon, your writings are divine,
And will live in the memories of your admirers until the end of time;
Your plays are read in family circles with wonder and delight,
While seated around the fireside on a cold winter's night.

Now I have finished.

Hans   I like the bit about the fireside on a cold winter's night.

Will   That is no consolation. What poetic gem have you to offer?

Hans   A moral tale. You see there was once a King who was absolutely insane about new clothes and one day, two swindlers came to sell him what they said was a magic suit of clothes. Now, they held up this particular garment and they said, "Your Majesty, this is a magic suit." Well, the truth of the matter is, there was no suit there at all. But the swindlers were very smart, and they said, "Your Majesty, to a wise man this is a beautiful raiment but to a fool it is absolutely invisible." Naturally, the King not wanting to appear a fool, said,

"Isn't it grand! Isn't it fine! Look at the cut, the style, the line!
The suit of clothes is all together
But all together it's all together
The most remarkable suit of clothes that I have ever seen.
These eyes of mine at once determined
The sleeves are velvet, the cape is ermine
The hose are blue and the doublet is a lovely shade of green.
Somebody send for the Queen."

Will   Aye, I imagine the Queen would get quite a surprise at tha'.

Hans   But no, she had heard it was only invisible to fools, so she also pretended to see it.

Will   More fool her.

Hans   Indeed. But there was a little boy who was not such a fool, and when he saw it he said,

"Look at the King! Look at the King! the King, the King, the King!
The King is in the all together
But all together the all together
He's all together as naked as the day that he was born.
The King is in the all together
But all together the all together
It's all together the very least the King has ever worn.
Call the court physician, call an intermission
His majesty is wide open to ridicule and scorn.
The King is in the all together
But all together the all together
He's all together as naked as the day that he was born.
And it's all together too chilly a morn!"

Will Well Mr Andersen, you certainly can put a canny little tale together, I grant ye – but it's not poetry. I'll wager in centuries to come when the name of William Topaz McGonagall is still on everybody's lips nobody will remember Hans Christian Andersen.

Hans We shall see. Time will tell, Mr McGonagall, time will tell. *(Exeunt)*

<u>**Act II Scene 4**</u> **Update** *(Front of Tabs)*

(Witch 1 & Gertrude enter through front tabs, dressed as cheer-leaders)

Witch 1 Are you going to tell them, or shall I?

Gertrude Tell what to whom?

Witch 1 Tell the spectators here. About the matches.

Gertrude You mean the fact that nobody has drowned. Yet.

Witch 1 Aye. That's a start.

Gertrude And that nobody except the Venetians knew the rules.

Witch 1 That too.

Gertrude And that somehow the Scots managed to beat the Venetians at their own game.

Witch 1 Inflatable sporrans – that was our secret weapon. They'd never seen the like before.

Gertrude While the Danes fought fiercely but fairly through the preliminary rounds, the quarter-finals and the semi-final…

Witch 1 To meet the Scots here in the final. The auld enemy. A rematch!

Gertrude Which we shall win this time.

Witch 1 Not a prayer.

Gertrude Inflatable sporrans have been banned from the final.

Witch 1 So have horns on helmets, which I notice you used to great effect against the Germans.

Gertrude They did not like it up them.

Witch 1 It was a sore point.

Gertrude But this game will be different. We will win fair and square.

Witch 1 That would be a first. The Scots are up for some action.

Gertrude Speaking of which, Witch, I think the action is about to start.

Witch 1 You mean, the teams are about to take the plunge.

Gertrude No more swanning about – they are about to get a ducking.

Witch 1 In at the deep end. Which is the deep end?

Gertrude *(Looking at the audience)* I think they are a bit shallow over there.

Witch 1 And more profound here, you mean?

Gertrude I am not so sure about that.

(The stage curtains open with a flourish)

Act II Scene 5 Match of the Bay *(Full Set and in auditorium)*

Witch 1 Oh-ho – here we go!

>Rah, Rah, hear our chant,
>Scots are great and Danes just aren't.

Gertrude Ya, Ya, yes we are,
>With our boats we travel far.

Witch 1 Hey, Hey, what we say,
>You're not using boats today.

*The teams enter wearing bathing gear
to a drowned version of 'Match of the Day' music*

Scottish team: Beth, Duncan, Macbeth, Banquo, Birnam, Glen, Morangie
Danish team: Polonius, Ophelia, Claudius, Horatio, Yorick, Carl, Berg
Between them: Witch 2, Portia, Witch 3

Portia Now the anthems.

Scottish Team: *Sing "Donald, where's your trousers"*

Danish Team: *Sing "We are sailing!"*

> *Portia blows her whistle and summons the team captains*
> *Duncan and Claudius for the toss*

Portia Now – you understand the rules?

Duncan We understand the rules of football, lassie, but we still dinna ken the rules of this flooded version.

Claudius The Danes are used to being <u>on</u> the water, not <u>in</u> the water.

Portia Only when your boats sink! – Sorry, they don't sink, do they.

Duncan So let's get this straight. If we drown a member of the opposition, it's a free kick to them, yes?

Portia It's a straight red card, drowning.

Claudius That keeps the numbers on each side even.

Portia Anyway, let's get started.

Duncan & Claudius Yes Miss!

Portia Jolly good. *(She tosses a coin)* Heads! Scots. That means I throw the ball to you first.

Duncan Are you getting in the water too?

Portia Golly, no. Do I look dressed for it? *(She does not!)* The ref has to stay land-side.

Claudius What about those witches running the line?

Portia They tell me they are going to hover above the water on their Nimbus Two Thousands. Does that mean anything to you?

Duncan Not a lot.

Portia Me neither – but that's witches for you. Are you ready for the off?

Duncan Are we ready to demolish the Danes again lads?

Scots Aye!

Claudius Are you Danes ready to sink the Scots?

Danes Ja, we are!

Portia Then into the water!

All except Portia, Gertrude & the Witches go down from the stage into the auditorium as if going into a swimming pool

Portia holds the ball, checks her watch and her lines-witches, blows her whistle and throws the ball to Macbeth The match begins.

Match to be choreographed!! Danes win.

Act II Scene 6 **Witches switch** *(Front of Tabs)*

(The three Witches appear through the front tabs)

Witch 1 I think it's fair to say that didn't quite go to plan.

Witch 3 Those Danes looked good in the water.

Witch 2 Be honest, the Scots were rubbish.

Witch 1 They didn't quite play to the standard we've come to expect…

Witch 2 They were rubbish.

Witch 3 The Danes had some lucky breaks – the Scots…

Witch 2 They were rubbish.

Witch 1 Well perhaps … You're right – they were rubbish.

Witch 3 Aye, they were rubbish.

Witch 1 So now the Danes want their trophy back.

Witch 2 Do we have one yet?

Witch 3 I think the competition is still in progress.

Witch 1 We'd better have one by the end of the show.

Witch 2 Or the Danes will get nasty.

Witch 3 Well, let them get nasty. Nasty Danes. Who cares?

Witch 1 They have the boat.

Witch 2 Oh aye, the boat.

Witch 3 What about the boat?

Witch 1 The boat the Scots need, to get home on.

Witch 2 If there's no trophy, the Danes might just row off and leave them here.

Witch 1 So I think we had better find a winner – down there somewhere.

Witch 2 Right. We need to collect them up.

Witch 3 Ready or not, we're coming!

(They descend into the auditorium)

Witch 1 And we'll tak them back to our coven for judging.

(Business with the audience as they collect the efforts & take them away)

<u>**Act II Scene 7**</u> **Back in the Venetian bar** *(Full Set)*

Kate is behind the bar. Entire cast on stage except for the Witches

Kate Last orders, please.

Glen Last orders?

Morangie Hey, these are medieval times. They didn't have last orders.

Banquo Will you no' let us drown our sorrows?

Kate There's a canal outside.

Banquo Thank you so much.

Birnam Are you treating the Danes the same as us?

Kate That depends on their manners.

Duncan Their manner is far too proud and haughty at the moment.

Macbeth You'd think they'd won fairly. That match was fixed from the start.

Hamlet Are you casting nasturtiums at the referee?

Ophelia I think you mean aspersions, Hammie. Nasturtiums are flowers, like the ones I had when I floated on the lake. Remember?

Hamlet By Millais! How could I forget the image? But weren't they rhododendrons?

Polonius I hate to spoil a good line in the script, but the flowers in his painting were actually, and incongruously, from an English riverside.

Macbeth This is all getting far too arty-farty for me. Anyway, I was casting nothing at the referee but the truth. The match was fixed.

Duncan Aye, we'd ask for a replay if we had the energy.

Claudius Nobody would give you a replay. The rules were fair and you did not obey them.

Duncan Oh, and I suppose bringing in the dolphin was fair?

Claudius Completely. There is no mention of dolphins in the rules.

Gertrude But the rules specifically forbade inflatable sporrans.

Macbeth Ha! They were not sporrans. They were your rowing knickers.

Beth We borrowed them for the occasion. You once suggested we should wear them.

Hamlet That was for rowing!

Macbeth But we found them so comfortable. And just right for wearing on the football pitch.

Duncan Leastways, on <u>this</u> football pitch.

Beth And the fact that they inflated and helped our boys to float…

Macbeth …is not our fault.

Gertrude It did you no good though. The ref made you take them off.

Duncan Aye – but we only agreed if she'd help us to do it!

Macbeth And she would have been up for it…

Beth …aye, if I hadn'a been there.

Macbeth Sadly…

Duncan …that's true.

(Portia has drifted into this conversation)

Portia Golly, are you boys trying to get me into trouble with FIFA?

Gertrude No trouble. You were magnificent.

Beth Says the trainer of the winning team.

Gertrude Portia is quite impartial. She is famed for it.

Hamlet She knows all about the quality of the Mersey.

Portia Oh yes, I do – it is not strained.

Glen Someone should warn the Mersey Docks & Harbour Board.

Morangie They'll be going through the motions already.

Polonius May I bring this scene to order please? It seems to be getting rather silly. And more to the point, where is our trophy? I thought there was to be a presentation to the winners directly after the match.

Beth Patience Polony…

Polonius And please do not call me Polony. It does not befit my office.

Ophelia Dad's office is very important to him. It is where he goes to have a snooze after lunch.

Polonius Who's side are you on, daughter?

Beth I don't care much what he does in his office. He can play table-top football or pocket billiards there for all I care – but he'll have to wait a wee while more for his trophy.

Polonius And I do not wish to be referred to in the third person while I am present.

Ophelia No, he gets really cross being referred to in the third person, doesn't he dad?

Polonius Pah! *(He wanders away to the other side of the set)*

Gertrude Ophelia, you should show more respect for your father.

Ophelia Serves him right. Pompous old…

Hamlet You are skating on thin ice, Feely. Or in the case of Venice, no ice at all!

Portia Gosh – I hope I'm not the cause of all this.

Beth Dinna fash yerself, lassie.

Portia What does that mean?

Macbeth "Don't wet yourself." It's highland talk.

Beth It means no such thing, man Mac, and ye know it.

Macbeth It must do – I googled it.

Beth I'll google you, if I don't poke you first – wi' my dagger!

Gertrude Who are bad losers now? We win the match, and you start fighting among yourselves. If we do not get our trophy very soon we will row away into the blue and leave you to swim home.

Glen There'll be no need for that. The trophy is on its way.

Morangie Actually, I'm told that several trophies are on their way.

(The Witches enter with several Trophies constructed by the audience)

Witch 1 Ta-rah!

Witch 2 Ta-rah!

Witch 3 Ta-rah!

Witch 1 We've worked our witchcraft on the bricks…

Witch 2 Before, they were a sorry mix…

Witch 1 But now you see we've taken pains…

Witch 3 To make them lovely for the Danes.

Witch 2 *(To Polonius)* Which one would you like?

Polonius Ladies – is this the best you can offer?

Witch 1 You should have seen them before.

Witch 3 Believe me, this is really quite an improvement.

Polonius Well, frankly I am not sure it is good enough.

Gertrude The one we gave you was a work of art. These are … not.

(Potential business with the audience)

Beth Well, it's what's on offer. Take it or leave it.

Gertrude You mean take it or leave you.

Macbeth We can manage without your little rowing boat. Don't think we can't.

Banquo How will we manage, boss?

Birnam It's a long way to swim.

Macbeth I said we can manage. Right, Dunc?

Duncan Right, Mac. Never rely on Danes.

Hamlet So, this is the parting of we, the eponymous pair.

Macbeth Looks that way, Hammie. I dare do all that may become a man.

Hamlet By your smiling, you seem to say so, Mac.

Portia *(Coming between them)* Take a pair of sparkling eyes.

Macbeth & Hamlet Pardon?

Portia Golly! Sorry, I thought we were still doing quotations.

Macbeth Aye, but that's nae the Bard.

Portia No?

Hamlet And it is time to go home. I am sure they would agree *(indicating the audience)*.

Portia I see. Well in that case I think I'll just pop back up the Po, to Parma. Ciao. *(She exits)*

Hamlet And we will row off to Elsinore. Farvel. Pity about the trophy. Have a nice swim. *(The Danes exit)*

Duncan Have a nice swim! Here's another nice mess you've gotten us into Macbeth! *(Blackout and sounds of thunder)*

Ach, sorry! I'd forgotten about the curse.

Beth Lights back please. Lights back!

> *(The lights do not return, but the Witches strike torches)*

Witch 1 The day has turned, the night is nigh.

Witch 2 Enough's enough, I hear you cry.

Witch 3 We've brought them here across the sea...

Witch 1 To see the sights of Italy.

Witch 2 But now they're stuck.

Witch 3 They're out of luck.

Witch 1 They've heard that all roads lead to Rome.

Witch 2 But that's not where they want to go. *(Lights snap on)*

Witch 3 *(To the audience)* So please, can you lot take them home?

All Witches Thank you kindly!

*** END OF BARD AGAIN! ***

Scots & Danes listen to Polonius pontificating

MacHamlet Goes West

And meets a Tempest

Part 3 of the MacHamlet trilogy

MacHamlet Goes West

Cast List

The Scottish Team:

Mac Macbeth .... opportunist goal-seeker

Beth Macbeth .... his wife, team director

Witch One (Morag) .... organiser of Scottish cheerleaders

Witch Two (Kirsty) .... a cheery cheerleader

Witch Three (Bella) .... a dour cheerleader

Duncan King .... team captain

Banquo the Ghost .... a phantom winger

Birnam Wood .... from where we get defence

Glen & Morangie .... supporters of the Scottish distilleries

The Danish Team:

Hamlet .... formerly known as Prince, dead ball specialist

Gertrude .... Hamlet's mother, team trainer, now married to Claudius

Claudius .... disputed team captain

Horatio .... a solid goalkeeper

Yorick .... good with the head

Polonius .... team manager

Ophelia .... team masseuse

Carl & Berg .... probably the best lager louts in the world

Prospero .... thinks he owns an island

Miranda .... his daughter fair

Caliban .... his servant

Ariel .... a clean fairy

*The year is 1056; which, as it happens, is the year before
Macbeth's untimely death in the Battle of Lumphanan.*

List of Scenes

Act I

Scene 1 The Witches convene *(Front of Tabs)*

2 In a Scottish pub *(Full Set)*

3 Witches wonder which way *(Front of Tabs)*

4 Scots prepare for the Cruise *(Half Set)*

5 On-board entertainment *(Full Set)*

6 The Witches make landfall *(Half Set)*

7 Cruise arrival *(Front of Tabs)*

8 On the beach *(Full Set)*

**** INTERVAL ****

Act II

Scene 1 Prospero & Polonius *(Front of Tabs)*

2 On the beach again *(Full Set)*

3 The Witches visit Prospero *(Half Set)*

4 Miranda's idea *(Front of Tabs)*

5 Beach Volleyball competition *(Full Set)*

6 Round-up *(Front of Tabs)*

7 Heading for home *(Full Set)*

Mac & Beth about to have a 'domestic'

MacHamlet Goes West

<u>**Act I Scene 1**</u> **The Witches convene** *(Front of Tabs)*

(The three witches declaim from different points in the auditorium, moving towards the stage.)

Witch 1 What brings us to this place again?

Witch 2 Why, Morag, you're the one to blame.

Witch 3 You sent a message, so we came. *(Holds up a scrap of paper)*

Witch 2 A coven in the Scottish rain.

Witch 1 I sent no message.

Witch 2   You did so. *(Holds up another scrap of paper)*

Witch 3 We both received it days ago.

Witch 2 It said to meet you here at eight.

Witch 3 Or thereabouts, but don't be late.

Witch 2 So here we are.

Witch 1   I sent no note.

Witch 3 Oh yes you did.

Witch 2 It came by boat.

Witch 3 It came ashore down by the dunes…

Witch 2 All neatly written out in runes.

Witch 1 In runes you say? I know that phrase.
You know who writes in runes these days.

Witch 3 The Danes who came to us before.

Witch 2 Perhaps we'd better lock the door!

Witch 3 There's no door, Kirsty.

Witch 2   What? Good grief!

Witch 3 We're standing on a blasted heath!

Witch 1 Dinna fash yerself. They're after Wags.
  They won't be wanting us old hags!

Witch 2 I'm not so sure that's true to say.
  We're quite bewitching in our way.

Witch 3 Wicked!

Witch 2   But I'd like to ken
  Why the Danes are back again.

Witch 1 Yes. There must be some good reason.

Witch 3 Maybe it's the football season!

Witch 2 Not again! Time's moving fast.
  It's fourteen years since we played last.

Witch 1 They'll have some different scam to sell us.

Witch 3 There's nothing in the runes to tell us.

Witch 1 But by the pricking of my thumbs,
  Something once more this way comes.
  Away, my sisters, and keep watch.

(The witches exit SL)

*(Hamlet enters SR to 'Air on a G string' and slowly starts to light up a small
  cigar. The stage manager enters quickly SR and takes the cigar.)*

Stage Manager No smoking. Don't you remember? *(The music stops)*

Hamlet I know, I know. It has not been discovered yet. But we mean to
  change all that.

Stage Manager You and whose army? *(Exits)*

Hamlet *(Looks at his watch)* Ah, 1056. Time for a little refreshment, I
  think, before my appointment. *(Takes out a can of Carlsberg)*

(Re-enter SL Witch 1)

Witch 1 So you're back again, and still on the gnat's water I see.

Hamlet We Danes have been brewing this for a very long time.

Witch 1 Without much improvement, in my opinion.

Hamlet It is *probably the best... (overlap with Witch 1)*

Witch 1 *...probably the best* lemonade in the world. I'll drink to that.

Hamlet Where I come from, that is fighting talk.

Witch 1 Where you come from anything is fighting talk. *(Holds up one of the scraps of paper)* You were the author of this, I assume.

Hamlet It is in my hand.

Witch 1 You wanted me to convene a coven.

Hamlet And are you fresh from the coven?

Witch 1 I am. But the coven is turned off at the moment.

Hamlet No cake then?

Witch 1 Pardon?

Hamlet If the coven is turned off.

Witch 1 I shall ignore that apology of a pun. The coven is turned off because the message was in runes, and we are not good at runes.

Hamlet Ah, in that case you need my patent Rune to Roman translator.

Witch 1 What's that?

Hamlet *(Holds up a largish Rubik's cube)* It is my runic cube. You line the runes up on one side and the translation appears on the other.

Witch 1 I see. Or rather, I don't.

Hamlet But you will see if you follow the instructions.

Witch 1 R–ight. Look, why don't you just tell me what the message is without having me fiddle around with your runes?

Hamlet That would ruin the story.

Witch 1 Enough! Are you going to tell me? – or am I going to turn around and go home?

Hamlet All right! We have started a new business, and we would like your Scottish people to be our first customers.

Witch 1 And all this rune stuff is your attempt at marketing?

Hamlet Well you have to admit it is different.

Witch 1 It's pathetic. Whose idea was it?

Hamlet You remember Ophelia?

Witch 1 Your little bit on the side? Yes, I remember her.

Hamlet She likes to travel.

Witch 1 So I've heard.

Hamlet In boats.

Witch 1 Oh, that too.

Hamlet And we have recently made discoveries in the West.

Witch 1 Bailey, Rockall, Shannon…

Hamlet Further west than that. We have found a New World.

Witch 1 To rape and pillage, no doubt.

Hamlet Madam, we have left all that behind. We are now responsible sea-farers.

Witch 1 Oh yes, since when?

Hamlet You have heard of Viking Cruises?

Witch 1 I don't watch daytime television repeats.

Hamlet Nor should you, even when they have been invented.

Witch 1 I'll bear that in mind. So, your Viking Cruises…

Hamlet Our Viking Cruises will transport you in unaccustomed luxury to the four corners of the world.

Witch 1 Four corners? Haven't we discovered that the world's round yet?

Hamlet Not if you want to stay friends with the Pope. But my corners are metaphorical.

Witch 1 Ah! Are we getting to the point yet?

Hamlet We need a Scottish representative if we are to sell the cruises here.

Witch 1 What's in it for us?

Hamlet Free holidays to exotic locations.

Witch 1 Balcony cabins?

Hamlet On a longship? I am afraid that is a luxury yet to come. Maybe a tarpaulin to cover you in a storm.

Witch 1 Sounds like it could be a difficult product to sell.

Hamlet It depends on what you are used to. And anyway…

Witch 1 Yes?

Hamlet They will not understand the brochure, because it will be in runes!

Witch 1 Clever! Now I see why you want to employ witches.

Hamlet Why is that?

Witch 1 To get a good review in the Witch report! *(They exit SL)*

Act I Scene 2 **In a Scottish pub** *(Full Set)*

The pub is populated with Scottish revellers.

Glen How long have we been propping up this bar now, Mac?

Macbeth Sixteen years this week, Glen.

Morangie That's a long, long time to be propping up a bar.

Macbeth Aye Morangie, but it would seem even longer if we didn't have the bar to prop up.

Glen That's true. And a decent dram to drink.

Morangie Remember those poor Danes when they were here? Drinking that strange liquid that looked like a horse had passed it.

Glen Did ye say 'passed' Morangie?

Morangie I did, Glen. I'm careful with my words, you know. They called it Lager.

Macbeth Sixteen years of good companionship.

Glen You're talking about the three of us, Mac. I don't think it's been an entirely good companionship we've had with some other people.

Morangie Your missus, for one.

Glen Aye, and devious Duncan for another.

Morangie Not to mention the Danes.

Macbeth No, please let's not mention the Danes.

Glen They brought some new ideas with them. Apart from lager, that is.

Macbeth Really?

Glen Remember those little coloured plastic bricks?

Macbeth Lego! They got smashed in my sporran. Not much use. Anything else?

Morangie Aye – the football game.

Glen And that female referee – remember her?

Morangie Good strip.

Glen You saw her in the altogether?

Morangie I mean the strip she wore. All in black. Suited her.

Macbeth She was from England, ye ken – not a Dane.

Glen Oh aye – Lady Godiva. She didn't stay.

Morangie Said she had to go and ride through Coventry with a bear. At least, I think that's what she said.

Glen Funny thing to do. Still, the English...

Macbeth Have you two stopped waffling on?

Glen Not much else to do these days, Mac.

Morangie Now all the raping and pillaging has been outlawed. Enough to drive a man to drink.

Macbeth Well, if you're buying – mine's the usual.

Glen We ought to get out more.

Macbeth That's what the wife keeps saying.

Morangie Aye, but where?

(Enter SL Beth, with a travel brochure)

Beth Well now, boys. I thought you'd be here.

Glen *(To Morangie)* Looks like we're about to find out.

Beth How would you like a wee trip out? Get you away from this smelly old bar.

Macbeth Last time we had a 'wee trip out' we ended up in – where was it? That place with rivers for roads. Where the football match turned into a water polo match.

Beth Venice. It was lovely.

Macbeth It was wet!

Beth You have no soul, Mac.

Macbeth Here I have a dram in my hand, and I'm warm and I'm dry.

Beth Well, I'm bored – and I've booked us all on a cruise.

Glen All?

Morangie On a what?

Beth This brochure appeared on my doorstep. Don't know where it came from, but it looks interesting.

Macbeth It looks like nothing on earth to me. What are all the little men?

Beth Mac, your education is sorely lacking. They are runes.

Macbeth Runes?

Glen Is that something you take when your nose is blocked?

Beth Danish writing.

Macbeth Not Danes again! Where are they?

Beth They come in peace. They are reformed. They are giving us the offer of a lifetime.

Macbeth They are untrustworthy villains.

Beth Their business is guaranteed.

Macbeth Guaranteed by who?

Beth Yes, I think that's right.

Macbeth What do you mean, 'that's right'? Who is it guaranteed by? Thor and Odin?

Beth No – those are the names of their boats. It's guaranteed by ABTA, whatever that is – and underwritten by The Doctor.

Morangie Not the one from the blue bothy with the flashing light on it?

Beth Aye, that's the one. That's who.

Glen You've already booked, you say.

Beth Seats were selling fast. I got the last seven places.

Macbeth You mean you've paid good groats for this? Already?

Beth I had to hurry. That's what they said.

Macbeth They? Who did you pay?

Beth A nice lady called Morag, and her two friends. Funny, I seem to have seen them before. Can't think where. Anyway, it's all fixed.

Macbeth Fixed sounds about right to me!

Beth Don't moan, man Mac. You'll love it. You'll all love it. We set sail tomorrow.

All men Tomorrow?

Beth Aye – first thing in the morning down at the harbour they said, to catch the tide. I'll go and pack. *(She exits SL)*

Macbeth *(To Glen)* Now look what you've done.

Glen Me? What did I do?

Macbeth "We ought to get out more" you said.

Glen Yes, but I didn't mean…

Macbeth Well, there's no stopping her now. We'd better tell the others.

(They begin to exit USR)

Morangie You can tell Duncan – I wouldn't dare.

Glen Banquo and Birnam won't be so bad. I'll tell them.

Morangie Only seven seats? McGonagall won't be coming then.

Glen We'll miss his odes.

Macbeth McGonagall? Oh no we won't!

(Curtain)

Act I Scene 3 **Witches wonder which way** *(Front of Tabs)*

(The three Witches enter SL)

Witch 1 So it's done. Our first clients are signed up.

Witch 2 Signed up, and paid up.

Witch 3 Who's next?

Witch 1 Well – nobody actually. There are only seven places for passengers on the boat – the other seats are occupied by the rowers.

Witch 3 So, we don't get to go along?

Witch 1 Well, that depends.

Witch 2 Depends on what?

Witch 1 Depends on where they're going to.

Witch 3 Don't they know where they're going to?

Witch 1 No – it's a bit of a mystery trip. They head west and hope the wind takes them somewhere interesting.

Witch 2 Is that what it said in the brochure?

Witch 1 It was mentioned somewhere in the small runes, I think.

Witch 3 So – we can go along if what?

Witch 1 We can go along if it's within our range. I'm talking broomsticks here, remember?

Witch 2 I only use mine to ride round to the herb garden now and then.

Witch 3 Mine's propping up the hovel wall – I ran out of building material.

Witch 2 Well it's lucky you didn't run out of firewood then!

Witch 1 Drag them out and dust them up. The brooms should be alright – it's our BTMs that I'm more concerned about.

Witch 3 We'd better find the soothing cream!

Witch 2 But Morag, if they don't know where they're going, how do we know where they're going?

Witch 1 We have technology, Kirsty.

Witch 2 We do?

Witch 1 Aye. In the brooms. The Doctor got them from that film studio, ye remember? We used them to fly to Italy.

Witch 3 But we knew where Italy was – or rather the brooms did.

Witch 1 The brooms come from a magical place in a future time. They'll know where to take us. And Who will be with us.

Witch 2 He will?

Witch 1 Trust me. I'm a travel agent – would I lie to you?

(They exit SL)

Act I Scene 4 **Scots prepare for the Cruise** *(Half Set)*

(The scene opens on six Scots packing)

Duncan Whose stupid idea was this anyway.

Glen We told you, Dunc, it was Beth – and the brochure.

Banquo You're not up for a bit of a holiday then, Dunc?

Duncan No, Banquo, I am not. But as Mac's wife is paying…

Macbeth What? Is she paying for everybody?

Morangie Well she's not asked us for money.

Macbeth Oh great! That'll all be coming out of my sporran then!

Birnam That's very generous of you, Mac.

Macbeth No, Birnam – it's very generous of my wife.

Morangie What are you packing, Glen?

Glen A spare kilt.

Morangie Just one spare kilt?

Glen Aye – it's good for all weathers. What more do you need?

Banquo Birnam was thinking of taking his bagpipes.

Duncan Birnam would.

Birnam I thought you might like a bit of musical entertainment on the trip.

Duncan What's musical entertainment got to do with your bagpipes?

Macbeth According to my wife, the brochure says there will be on-board entertainment provided.

Duncan That's all good then. You can leave the bagpipes in your hovel.

Banquo The sight of them should frighten off intruders while we're away.

Birnam Does anyone know how long we'll be away?

Macbeth The brochure seems a bit vague. Just says 'the experience of a lifetime'. Doesn't say how long the lifetime might be.

Birnam If the boat goes down it could be quite a short one.

Duncan Thank you Birnam – we're trying not to think of it.

Banquo I tried swimming once.

Glen Where was that, Banquo?

Banquo In the village pond, when I slipped in.

Morangie How did you manage?

Banquo Not very well – I had to be rescued.

Glen You wouldn't stand a ghost of a chance in the middle of the sea then.

Macbeth Can we stop all this – it's giving me a sinking feeling.

(Beth enters SL)

Beth How are we doing, boys? All packed and ready to go?

Duncan You've a lot to answer for here Macbeth.

(Blackout and sounds of thunder)

Beth Well that's not very clever of you Duncan. You should remember our name strikes fear into the very fabric of theatrical society. Can we have our lights back again please?

(The lights come back on)

Beth Thank you kindly.

Duncan What am I supposed to call him – Mr Scottish Play?

Macbeth You can call me Mac like everyone else does, Dunc.

Duncan Don't call me Dunc. It's demeaning.

Macbeth Alright, I'll call you Demeaning then.

Duncan Pah!

Beth Boys, boys – enough is enough. The waggon's outside to take your bags down to the boat – and now you need a good night's rest.

Glen Waggon? Who needs a waggon? I can carry my spare kilt in my shoulder bag.

Morangie Aye, me too. *(All the other men agree with this in their own way)*

Beth Oh, fine – there'll be plenty of room on the waggon for my twelve cases then. Come on Mac – time for bed!

(She leads him off SL – as they go...)

Glen I thought you said he needed a good night's rest Beth.

(Curtain)

Act I Scene 5 On-board entertainment *(Full Set)*

(Starts Front of Tabs – Polonius and Ophelia enter DSL)

Polonius So, daughter, you have been nominated Chief Entertainments Officer for this cruise.

Ophelia Yes dad.

Polonius And what does that involve actually?

Ophelia Er, keeping the customers entertained, I imagine.

Polonius So that would be: quiz games, bingo, line dancing… that sort of thing?

Ophelia That sort of thing. And pole dancing.

Polonius I beg your pardon, daughter. What is pole dancing?

Ophelia You dance – round a pole. There is a big mast in the middle of the boat   that should do.

Polonius I dance round a pole?

Ophelia No, dad, not you. That is my job.

Polonius I see – or rather, I do not really see.

Ophelia No, and you might not want to see – but the customers should be entertained by it. Except for Mrs Mac, though she might learn a thing or two.

Polonius Oh well, that is alright then. Shall we go and see how the rest of the staff are doing?

(The curtains open to reveal on-board entertainments)

Gertrude Ah, there you are Polonius. We are needing your advice.

Claudius Gertrude and I were discussing the formalities for sitting at the Captain's table.

Polonius The Captain's table?

Claudius Indeed. I am the Captain of this vessel and I wish to welcome my guests in the traditional style.

Gertrude We have heard that the Captain should entertain his guests to a formal dinner.

Polonius I see. But where is there space to put a table? And to seat all your guests at once.

Gertrude That is our problem, Polonius. It seems that the boat was not designed with luxury cruises in mind.

Polonius True, madam. It was designed for warfare. Accommodation is at a premium. You may remember that when this venture into cruising was first mentioned I did hold out some reservations…

Claudius Yes, yes. But Hamlet went ahead and arranged the business anyway, so now we are stuck with it.

Gertrude Actually, Claudius quite likes the idea. He gets to wear a fancy uniform with epaulettes.

Polonius Amazing.

Claudius You do not sound very impressed, Polonius.

Ophelia I think daddy is wondering how the fancy uniform will survive several weeks in an open boat.

Polonius I was thinking of that and much, much more, daughter.

Gertrude So, back to the table…

Polonius I will give it my most earnest consideration, madam.

Claudius And now I must go for my fitting. We have found a local seamstress who seems to know what to do.

Gertrude Nice girl, name of Morag. Quite bewitching.

(Claudius and Gertrude exit SL)

Polonius Morag. I seem to have heard that name before.

Ophelia Quite likely, daddy. Half the girls in Scotland are named Morag.

Polonius Yes, but I have my suspicions over this one…

Ophelia Now, what are Horatio and Yorick up to?

Polonius They appear to be manufacturing some square cards.

Horatio It is the Bingo you asked for, Ophelia.

Yorick We are building the houses.

Ophelia Building the houses?

Yorick For the numbers to go in.

Horatio And when you fill the houses with numbers you shout 'Bingo!'

Polonius This is entertainment?

Ophelia Better than just sitting watching the sea, I am told.

Polonius I think I would rather be chained to an oar, rowing like a true Viking.

Ophelia At your age we should not let you anywhere near an oar.

Polonius You think I am incapable of pulling an oar, daughter?

Ophelia I was not referring to your private life, father.

Polonius Neither was I. With an oar through my rowlocks I will perform like the best of them.

Carl Ophelia, we are having an argument over here.

Berg You must help us.

Ophelia Thank goodness for that – the conversation with my father was getting embarrassing!

Carl It is about these quizzes that we are supposed to be organising.

Berg Carl thinks they should be made difficult.

Carl I do. What is the pleasure in always knowing the answers? Berg thinks we should pander to the less intelligent. I do not agree with him.

Ophelia Give me an example of a difficult question.

Carl If I am in a barrel, I make it lighter. What am I?

Ophelia Hot air?

Berg That is what Carl is – a lot of hot air!

Carl But it is not the correct answer.

Ophelia I give up – what is it in a barrel that makes it lighter?

Carl A hole! It is not so difficult – just needs a bit of thinking about.

Ophelia Pah! So, Berg, what would an easy question be?

Berg Who is the Captain of this ship?

Ophelia That is a very good question, but I do not think there is an easy answer.

Polonius Indeed. I think you could start a mutiny by asking that question.

Berg The answer is obviously Claudius, is it not?

Ophelia I do not think Hammie would agree with you there.

Polonius I am sure he would not. But he can tell you himself.

(Enter Hamlet SR)

Hamlet What is it I can I tell you myself?

Ophelia Who is the Captain of this ship?

Hamlet It is I. This is the captain of your ship …

Ophelia Your heart speaking!

Hamlet It is my head speaking, Feely. It is a young man's job.

Polonius Will you stop calling my daughter Feely. She is Ophelia, Ophelia.

Hamlet Bless you!

Polonius And I do not think it is a young man's job. Much experience is needed to guide a boat across the seas. A knowledge of the stars for a start.

Hamlet I am told I am a ram.

Ophelia Well, lucky me!

Polonius I am not talking about signs of the zodiac.

Ophelia Neither were we!

Polonius This conversation is becoming unbecoming for a father. I shall leave. Remember you have a job to do, Ophelia, and preferably before our guests arrive. *(He exits SR)*

Carl Whoops!

Ophelia Oh, do not mind my father – he is like it all the time.

Berg Anyway, I think we have finished our bit.

Hamlet And Horatio and Yorick look as if they have too, so we are ready for the boarding party. Put your hat on straight, Feely. *(There is the sound of a bosun's whistle)* Here they come now.

(The Scots enter SL: Macbeth, Beth, Duncan, Glen, Morangie, Banquo & Birnam – Beth has much medieval luggage)

Macbeth Do we have to show our tickets?

Ophelia Welcome aboard the good ship *Thor*. I am Ophelia, your Entertainments Officer. We hope your stay will be a pleasant one, but if you do have any problems, just let me know and I shall do my best to put them right.

Glen Do you have any problems for her to put right, Morangie?

Morangie I could think of a few things I'd like her to put right, Glen.

Beth Boys! Be respectful to the staff please.

Hamlet And I am your Captain.

Duncan You look a wee bit young to be a Captain, laddie. Are you sure you know the ropes?

Hamlet Ropes?

Beth Perhaps you could show us to our quarters.

Hamlet Quarters?

Beth You know – our accommodation. Where we are to sleep, and store our luggage.

Hamlet Luggage? Well...

Ophelia Let me handle this Hammie. You go and make sure the ship is ready to row away.

Hamlet To row. Right. *(Shouts)* All Danes, to your rowing positions!

(The Danes move stools to their rowing positions during the next lines)

Beth But I don't see our cabins.

Ophelia The *Thor* has been recently fitted with all the most modern features of the age. There is a seawater shower at the bow; a canvas storm shelter near the stern; a seat projecting over the side for your convenience...

Beth A what? You mean a midden.

Ophelia You cannot have a midden on a ship. You have to do it over the side. It is an exhilarating feeling, especially in a storm.

Macbeth I think the gents have a wee advantage there, dear.

Beth Thank you, Mac – you're not helping. Any other features of the age?

Ophelia There is a happy hour at sunset.

Glen You mean the rest of the time we're unhappy?

Morangie How much did we pay for this?

Beth You didn't – I did. *(To Ophelia)* So, no cabin then.

Ophelia I am sorry – it is the medieval times we live in. One day there will be cabins.

Duncan Which day would that be?

Banquo No time soon by the looks of it.

Birnam I'd be better off in my hovel.

Duncan Well, thank you kindly Beth, but I think I'm going home.

Banquo Me too.

Birnam And me.

(At this moment we hear instructions shouted and we see the Danes start rowing – they keep this up till the end of the scene)

Beth Too late – we're off. Unless you fancy a swim.

Ophelia I can arrange for a chest to keep your belongings in – to keep them dry.

Macbeth One chest between all of us?

Ophelia The *Thor* is one of our smaller vessels – we call it our bijou option. Space is rather limited.

Beth So, one chest between all of us. *(She looks at her luggage)*

Glen I've no problem with that – I've only my spare kilt.

Morangie Same here. That and the odd bottle of whisky.

Macbeth I think it's you who have the problem, Beth.

Duncan Quarts into a pint pot come to mind.

Beth I shall cope – don't you worry. Perhaps some of you men would help me carry these bags to the chest.

Ophelia I will lead the way.

(Ophelia leads Beth & Glen, Morangie, Banquo & Birnam carry her bags to exit SR)

Duncan Women!

Macbeth She's a mind of her own and no mistake. It's murder if she's crossed.

Duncan Aye, so I remember. So, where are we headed for in this boat?

Macbeth The brochure says to 'the exotic land of the setting sun', wherever that is. And it could take a few days.

Duncan A few days you say? With only the fish and these Danes for

127

company until we get there?

Macbeth Let's hope we've brought enough whisky to last the voyage.

Duncan I've a dram or two we can share in my sporran.

Macbeth Share in your sporran? There's an offer I don't hear often!

Duncan Aye, well make the most of it while it's there. I don't open my sporran for just anybody.

Macbeth I will. And in the meantime – d'you fancy a game of Bingo?

(The curtains close)

First Interval if you are serving a 2-course meal to the audience

<u>**Act I Scene 6**</u> **The Witches make landfall** *(Half Set)*

(The scene begins Front of Tabs)

(The Witches fly in through the auditorium on their broomsticks)

Witch 1 This is where they're headed for.

Witch 2 The exotic land of the setting sun? Is this it?

Witch 3 Looks like curtains to me!

Witch 1 Yes, but exotic curtains, don't you think?

Witch 2 No – they look like fairly ordinary curtains to me.

Witch 3 Me too.

Witch 1 Well, maybe there's something exotic behind them.

Witch 2 Or maybe we're miles off course. What makes you think it's here anyway?

Witch 1 I have a nose for it.

Witch 3 You can say that again!

Witch 1 And wherever my nose goes, I follow.

Witch 2 Does it now? Well there's a novelty!

Witch 1 And right now, my nose goes through those curtains.

Witch 3 To the exotic land of the setting sun.

Witch 2 *(Sighs)* Oh well, we'll find out when we get there I suppose. Here goes.

(They approach the curtains, which open on a scene of desolation)

Witch 3 So, this is the exotic land of the setting sun?

Witch 2 About as exotic as my hovel.

Witch 1 Ladies, do not give up so soon. My nose tells me that we have arrived.

Witch 2 Well obviously we have arrived. But where?

(Desert Island Discs theme begins)

Witch 3 Oh-ho! Sounds like your cue, Kirsty.

Witch 2 Aye, well. My castaway this week is – three ladies from Scotland who got lost on their broomsticks while crossing the Western sea…

Witch 1 Ok, so we're on a desert island. We get the message – you can cut the music now.

(Music stops)

Witch 3 Just as well – I haven't thought of the records I want played.

Witch 2 And we certainly don't want the complete works of Shakespeare!

(Enter Ariel SL)

Ariel Did somebody call?

Witch 1 Who are you?

Ariel I am one of the most complete works of Shakespeare.

Witch 2 Well, we're pretty complete works of Shakespeare ourselves.

Ariel Hmm – nice besoms by the way. Which one are you?

Witch 2 No, I'm Witch 2. This *(indicating Morag)* is Witch 1.

Witch 3 And I'm Witch 3 – how do you do.

Witch 1 We are from the play that dare not speak its name.

Ariel You mean – Macbeth?

(Blackout and massive storms linger before lights return)

Witch 2 Hey! That's impressive.

Witch 3 We don't get storms like that in Scotland.

Ariel You don't have Tempests?

Witch 1 No, we came along before he thought of The Tempest. He was still in his 'eye of newt and toe of frog' period.

Ariel Pity. It's great fun controlling the weather. You should try it.

Witch 2 How about some hot, dry summers in Scotland?

Witch 3 Anything to get rid of the clegs and midges.

Ariel We can do hot and dry if we want to – but right now I've been asked to brew up a storm for this ship that's approaching.

Witch 1 Our ship?

Ariel Is it your ship? We thought it belonged to some fierce and shaggy Norsemen.

Witch 2 Fierce and shaggy? That will be their pillaging and raping you're referring to. No, they gave that up a few years back.

Witch 3 Took to playing football instead.

Witch 2 Though, to be fair, we didn't notice too much difference.

Witch 1 We have – acquaintances – on the ship.

Ariel Can they swim?

Witch 3 Only with armbands.

Ariel Then we may have a problem. I've been asked to wreck the ship.

Witch 1 Just a wee minute – why have you been asked to wreck the ship?

Ariel My master likes his solitude.

Witch 2 Bit extreme, isn't it? Wrecking every ship that comes along.

Ariel Well, to be honest, there are very few that ever come here. We're not on the maps, you see.

Witch 1 That's not surprising – there are no maps yet. So, who is this master of yours?

Ariel He goes by the name of Prospero.

Witch 3 *(Consulting a book she's found)* Italian nobleman turned into a wizard, daughter Miranda, servant Caliban and...

Witch 1 Whoa Bella! – where's all this from?

Witch 3 The Complete Works – it was hidden here all the time. This must be Ariel.

Ariel Can't deny it. Clean as a whistle. One of four fresh fairies.

Witch 3 There's only you in the book.

Ariel The Bard is not infallible. He missed out Tide, Surf and Dreft.

Witch 2 He'll be missing his two most famous characters if this wrecking goes ahead.

Witch 1 Aye – with Mac and Hamlet both gone, what's left?

Witch 3 It's alright – they survive the shipwreck.

Witch 1 Who do?

Witch 3 The people on the ship do. It says so here.

Ariel Huh! People will keep reading ahead!

Witch 2 And now, would you like to choose your first record?

Ariel Pardon? The isle is full of noises.

Witch 2 You are the castaway here?

Witch 1 Not now, Kirsty. We need a word with this Prospero first. *(To Ariel)* Where do we find him?

Ariel Come unto these yellow sands, and then take hands. *(Exits SL)*

Witch 3 He's quoting again!

Witch 1 I'll forgive him that if he gets us to see his boss. Hitch up your besoms, girls. We're off to see the wizard!

(They follow Ariel off – curtains close)

Act I Scene 7 **Cruise arrival** *(Front of Tabs)*

(We hear the sounds of great storms and shipwreck. Danes and Scots 'swim' through the auditorium clinging to various floatation devices.)

Duncan I told you he wasn't fit to captain a boat.

Gertrude It was an easy mistake to make.

Macbeth He was too close to the shore – trying to show off.

Beth I've lost all my luggage.

Macbeth Aye, well that's about the only good thing to have come out of it.

Claudius He was not supposed to be Captain. I was supposed to be captain.

131

Duncan Then you would have wrecked the ship instead of him – what's the difference?

Beth Call yourself sailors? I thought Danes could handle anything.

Hamlet I have never seen waves so big. It was not natural. Where is Feely?

Ophelia I am here, looking after father.

Polonius Leave me, daughter – I am frail. I would not want to drag you down.

Hamlet Do not worry, Polony – she has natural buoyancy.

Duncan So we've noticed.

Macbeth Perhaps she'd like to teach me the breast stroke.

Duncan Careful, Mac, your wife's looking daggers at you.

Beth I'll teach you to crawl first, husband – along the seabed if necessary!

Hamlet My feet are touching the ground.

Claudius That is a first – your head is usually in the clouds.

Hamlet This way, Feely. The water is more shallow here.

Claudius It must be a reef.

Gertrude No – I believe it is a flight of steps.

Beth Up to a landing stage.

Hamlet I said I would bring you safely to land.

Beth You didn't say it would be without luggage or a ship though.

(They all drag themselves one by one onto the stage)

Claudius Some of you go and search for firewood – we need to dry out.

(Carl, Berg, Horatio, Yorick, Glen, Morangie, Birnam & Banquo exit SR & SL)

Macbeth So this is 'the exotic land of the setting sun'.

Hamlet I am sure it will be, once we start exploring.

Duncan Aye. Where do we go from here?

Ophelia Daddy would like to go somewhere quite quickly.

Polonius That information was not for general circulation, daughter.

Ophelia No, but when you have to go, you have to go. Perhaps behind these drapes?

(Polonius sneaks furtively through the curtains)

He is getting on a bit now, you know.

Duncan Aye, it comes to us all in the end.

Beth Well, I'm not standing around here all day. If this is an exotic cruise destination, I want to find out where it all happens.

(At that moment, the curtains open revealing Polonius caught short)

Oh, I didn't quite mean that!

(Ophelia moves to shield him)

Ophelia Oops! Sorry, daddy.

Act I Scene 8 On the beach *(Full Set)*

(We find ourselves on a desert island – the action is continuous)

(Enter Caliban SL – he is dressed as a beach attendant)

Caliban Hey you! We don't do that sort of thing around here.

Claudius That is no way to address a lady.

Caliban I wasn't addressing the lady – I was addressing the undressed gent.

Ophelia That is no gent – that is my father.

Caliban Then he oughta know better. Hasn't he heard of water closets?

Beth Have you heard of a dagger in your gizzard?

Caliban Are you disrespecting me?

Beth Probably, if I knew what it meant.

Caliban Careful. I can give on-the-spot fines, you know.

Hamlet And we can give on-the-spot lessons in butchery. Do you know who we are?

Caliban Why, have you forgotten?

Hamlet That is a very old joke and was not funny even when it was young.

Macbeth *(With dirk)* How would you like to die?

Caliban Well, if it's anything like yesterdie, not very much.

Gertrude Boys, boys. This is no way to begin our holiday.

Duncan He started it.

Gertrude We may need his help.

Beth Aye, that's true.

Claudius *(To Caliban)* Are you going to tell us where we can get shelter?

Caliban I don't have to do this job, you know.

Beth Are you not happy in your work?

Caliban Up before sunrise to clean the beach. Unlock the water closets for people who won't use them. Get the deck chairs ready for tourists who never turn up. I wouldn't mind if I was paid a decent wage...

Beth We'll take that as a 'no' then.

Caliban And then there's the evening work. My master likes his meals served on time. And all cooked from fresh. And the mistress too.

Hamlet He likes his mistress cooked from fresh?

Ophelia You would not like your mistress cooked from fresh, would you Hammie?

Hamlet No, Feely, I prefer her with the chill just taken off.

Ophelia Hmmm – just the chill?

Caliban And there's all the fetching and carrying – and did you mention a holiday? I don't know what one of those is.

Gertrude Alright, alright, enough already! We are sorry we bothered you. We will get out of your hair if you tell us where we can find some accommodation.

Caliban Accommodation.

Gertrude Yes.

Caliban You want accommodation.

Claudius If you would be so kind.

Beth You do have accommodation here, don't you?

Gertrude For all these tourists you mentioned.

Caliban There were plans once...

Macbeth Plans?

Caliban The master's cave would have made a wonderful holiday apartment. The mountain air, the views out to sea…

Hamlet Would have made?

Caliban But we never got the visitors, you see.

Macbeth Aye, because there was no accommodation, ye ken.

Caliban No, because of the storms.

Hamlet It was not just us? Others have been wrecked here?

Caliban Too right. My fault really.

Gertrude Your fault?

Caliban Yes. I taught the master a few magic tricks I'd learned from my mother, and before I knew it – poof!

Claudius What is this 'poof'?

Caliban That's the master taking my magic and making it his own. With knobs on.

Ophelia What was that about his knobs?

Hamlet Calm down, Feely. It is not what you think it is.

Ophelia Magic with knobs sounds cool to me.

Caliban My mother could make rain, but the master wasn't satisfied until he could let loose a hurricane. Not good for business.

Beth So, no accommodation then.

Duncan Where is this master of yours? Perhaps we should meet him.

Caliban He'll be around – in his own good time. Him and his daughter.

Duncan Sounds a bit casual to me.

Beth This really is not good enough.

Macbeth *(To Beth)* Now just remind me – who was it chose this trip?

Beth It looked fine in the brochure.

Duncan The brochure the Danes gave us.

Polonius Forgive my intrusion, but I think you will find that the cruise was sold to you by a third party.

Hamlet Ah, Polony, you are back from inspecting the grass. Welcome to the party.

Polonius I have told you before, do not call me Polony.

Ophelia Hammie, control yourself. This is not the time nor the place to be needling my father. We are facing a crisis. We need cool heads.

Gertrude Well said, Ophelia. That is how to handle my son.

Hamlet She knows very well how to handle me, thank you mother.

Polonius *(To Duncan)* I believe you will find that any claims you may have will be with that party, not with the shipping agent.

Duncan Are you trying to wriggle out of your responsibilities here?

Polonius I am merely stating the terms, conditions and exclusions under which the contract was agreed.

Beth Look, while you're all arguing, I'm freezing to death here. What we need is a plan.

Macbeth What we need is a miracle.

Caliban Well, you're getting the next best thing – the master has arrived.

(Enter Prospero and Miranda SR)

Prospero Our revels now are ended. We are such stuff as dreams are made on.

Beth Are you the master?

Prospero I am Prospero, master of a full poor cell.

Miranda O, wonder! How many goodly creatures are there here! How beauteous mankind is! O brave new world, that has such people in't!

Macbeth Say that again?

Prospero This is my daughter, Miranda.

Macbeth Well, that <u>is</u> a miracle.

Hamlet A miracle of womanhood, would you not say Mac?

Beth Thank you, boys – I think we also-rans of womanhood can handle this nicely.

Ophelia Yes, Hammie – I hope you are not thinking of being fickle here.

Beth *(To Prospero)* Your daughter, you say.

Miranda Yes, I am his daughter.

Gertrude A woman who speaks for herself. I like that.

Claudius So we have noticed.

Miranda But I am not used to meeting people. My father keeps them from me.

Duncan Shame!

Miranda You are the first to have survived the tempest.

Macbeth Aye, well I'm told it's not the Bard's most popular play.

Hamlet I can well believe some have not survived it.

Miranda You are the first to have walked these sands.

Duncan No wonder your beach attendant was looking glum!

Miranda Oh, Caliban – yes, he doesn't get much custom either.

Prospero There were very good reasons for this.

Macbeth To keep marauding Danes off your shore, I suppose.

Hamlet More likely to keep vagrant Scotsman from your daughter.

Prospero But I have since been persuaded to open up my private island…

Duncan That's good!

Prospero …but only under strict terms and conditions.

Miranda And exclusions.

Prospero Yes: terms, conditions and exclusions.

Claudius Which are?

Prospero First, you come only on a cruise organised by a reputable agency.

Gertrude Our agency is most reputable. It came top of the Witch list.

Prospero Second, you do not disturb the flora or fauna of the island.

Polonius That means the plants and animals.

Hamlet Thank you, Polony – we are not uneducated.

Macbeth It's all Greek to me!

Hamlet No, Latin actually – I know these things.

Prospero Third…

Beth How long is this list?

Prospero Third and last… my daughter has a favour to ask.

Beth *(Suspicious)* What kind of favour?

Ophelia She is altogether too glamorous for my liking.

Gertrude Ours are rough men to be giving her favours.

Prospero The favour will be given by you all.

Ophelia Kinky!

Hamlet I do not think this man follows your line of thought, Feely.

Prospero But for the moment, I will not reveal it…

Duncan That's a relief.

Prospero The favour, that is.

Miranda My father does like to build up the suspense.

Prospero So after you and your friends have refreshed yourselves, I shall return. Come Miranda, Caliban – we will leave them for an interval. *(They begin to exit)* Oh, and by the way, if there is a raffle, make sure I get a winning ticket.

(They exit SR as the curtain falls)

*** INTERVAL ***

<u>**Act II Scene 1**</u> **The Great Debate** *(Front of Tabs)*

(Enter SL Polonius & Prospero together)

Prospero Good master Polonius, you and I are of an age and gravity to discuss the world in which we find ourselves.

Polonius Indeed, good master Prospero. Away from the hot heads and hearts of those around us.

Prospero And, for me, it is a rare opportunity to be able to speak with another of my own standing.

Polonius Shakespeare certainly placed you in a lonely station.

Prospero And we both have daughters to worry about.

Polonius Ah! That is most certainly true. I shudder to think what Ophelia gets up to half the time.

Prospero Whereas my Miranda has no-one to get involved with. Other than my servant Caliban.

Polonius Until now.

Prospero My point precisely. I was waiting for a certain Italian prince to turn up.

Polonius And sweep her off her feet?

Prospero I would give him some challenges to complete first, of course, to prove his love. As one does.

Polonius I think Hamlet is beyond performing any challenges. I sometimes arrange myself behind the arras to see if there is method in his madness – and wonder what will happen next.

Prospero But now you have brought the hirsute compliment of two plays to my shores. This upsets greatly the balance of my plans for her.

Polonius You think she will not be minded to wait for the Italian prince?

Prospero He may indeed have missed his opportunity.

Polonius But the Bard will surely bar any interference with his plots.

Prospero Your very presence here informs us otherwise. Be warned, there is magic afoot which is not of our making.

Polonius You have evidence of this?

Prospero My sprite Ariel has late brought me news of three Scottish ladies arrived on the island. He says they flew here.

Polonius They flew?

Prospero He is bringing them to see me. I believe one of them may be called Morag.

Polonius Morag – that name again.

Prospero I will go now and let you know what happens at our meeting. *(Exits SR)*

Polonius Thank you. *(Gives a Vulcan salute)* Live long and prosper-o. *(Exits SL)*

Act II Scene 2 On the beach again *(Full Set)*

(There is now a bar as in Act I set up on the beach.
It is populated with the Danes and Scots)

Glen This is more like it, Morangie!

Morangie Aye, Glen. Back at the bar wi' a dram in my hand. We could almost be in Scotland.

Carl It was good that we used crates of lager as ballast on the ship.

Berg And we needed much ballast.

Glen Luckily we had a few crates of whisky too which mysteriously floated ashore.

Morangie So everybody's happy – Skol!

Carl Sláinte.

Berg Well, in fact Claudius is not very happy.

Glen Oh, why's that?

Berg He has no longer a boat to be captain of.

Morangie You mean it's a wee bit shorter now since it hit the rocks.

Berg And we may have to stay here for a while.

Glen There's no hardship in that, while there's sunshine, sand and a well-stocked bar.

Morangie None whatsoever.

(Enter Ophelia SR)

Ophelia Well, boys, are you ready for some games.

Duncan Games? What sort of games would those be lassie?

Hamlet Feely has many games up her jumper.

Macbeth I'll be in trouble wi' the wife if she has.

Ophelia We have the Bingo, we have themed quizzes…

Duncan Not more of those, for heaven's sake!

Horatio How about a sand castle competition?

Yorick We could build a model of Elsinore.

Banquo Aye and we could do one of Cawdor.

Birnam Not so many fancy spires as Elsinore. Should be easier.

Ophelia Well, if that is your fancy…

Duncan No, but it may have to do.

Ophelia I am told to the east there is fine yellow sand.

Macbeth So long as it's not too far away from the bar.

(The men exit SR with buckets & spades)

Ophelia And what can we do for the ladies?

Gertrude I think we two ladies can look after ourselves, thank you Ophelia.

Beth Take your hat off – come and join in the gossip. You've no need to be on duty now.

Gertrude Although a piña colada would be nice if you are passing the bar.

Ophelia I think you will have to wait a few centuries for that.

Beth I wonder what the weather's like in Scotland now. I could get used to this.

Gertrude Denmark will be dreary. It is why we like to travel.

(Enter Caliban SL with three deck chairs)

What is this? It is that man again.

Beth Aye, and he seems to be struggling with a strange contraption.

Gertrude I think he needs some help, Ophelia.

(Ophelia goes to help Caliban)

Caliban Bless you, madam. It's many a year since I had to bring these out.

Ophelia What are these?

Caliban Well – chairs. I thought you might like to sit on them. It's what they're for.

Gertrude Chairs?

Beth How d'you make that into chairs?

Caliban Three chairs, madam. They separate from each other – somehow. And then they unfold – as I recall.

Ophelia As you recall?

Caliban Yes, well, as I say, it's been a long time… I may need some assistance.

Gertrude Ophelia, you are good with your hands.

Beth This should be interesting to watch.

(Business as Caliban and Ophelia try to put up a deck chair)

Ophelia Who would like to be the first to sit on it?

Gertrude You are the customer on our cruise, Beth. You should be the first.

Beth You're too kind.

(Business as Beth tries to sit in the chair)

Beth I'm in – I think.

Gertrude Is it comfortable?

Beth Aye, but I'm not sure how I'm going to get out.

Ophelia You just relax. We will worry about that later.

Caliban There is a small charge for use of the chairs.

Gertrude What?

Caliban Same on all the beaches on the island. Standard charge.

Beth But you don't have any visitors, you said.

Caliban It's the rules.

Ophelia Can you not relax the rules this once. We did help you put the chair up.

Caliban *(Sucks teeth)* More than my job's worth. Rules are rules.

Gertrude So, how much is it we have to pay?

Caliban Let's see. We're in high season and it's a weekend afternoon – that will be two ducats.

Beth Wha' in the Bard's name is a ducat?

Caliban A ducat is a weekday morning out of season.

Ophelia I think that is what my father would call a recursive argument.

Gertrude Well I for one will sit on a crate rather than pay.

Ophelia Me too.

Beth But I canna get out of it.

Ophelia Do not worry – Viking Cruises will pay for you.

Beth No, I mean I canna get out of the chair!

Gertrude Ophelia, you take one hand...

(Together Gertrude & Ophelia extract Beth from the chair)

And now, Signor Jobsworth, you can haul your chairs back to the stack. We will do without.

Caliban I don't have to do this job, you know.

Gertrude Yes, you told us before.

Beth And that's alright, because now you don't have to.

Caliban *(On his way out SL with the chairs)* 'The clouds methought would open, and show riches ready to drop upon me.' But that only happens in plays.

Ophelia Were we too cruel to him?

Gertrude He would not survive in one of our plays.

Beth Nobody survives in our plays.

Gertrude Well none of us do anyway.

Ophelia Excuse me, we are on holiday. Can we change the subject? Anyway, look, the boys are back from building their sand castles.

(The men re-enter SR)

How did it go?

Hamlet It did not go well, Feely. The Scots attacked our castle unfairly – with water.

Macbeth What good's a castle that canna withstand a shower of rain?

Hamlet A shower? It was a tidal wave. It would have sunk a longship.

Macbeth So then the they flattened our fortress. It was not designed to withstand an attack by full-size Danes.

Hamlet Nothing withstands an attack by full-size Danes.

Beth So I take it there is nothing left for us to come and see.

Ophelia Oh well, there will be no prizes awarded for that game then.

Macbeth Prizes?

Hamlet Nobody mentioned prizes!

Ophelia It is too late now. The damage is done.

Gertrude That is boys for you.

Beth Too true! So what now?

Ophelia I was thinking a barbecue on the beach tonight? To celebrate our first day on the island.

Gertrude Do you think Jobsworth will try to charge us for that too?

Beth If he does, he might find himself skewered by my dagger and becoming the main course.

Macbeth That's my wife – always ready to economise on the meat bill.

(The curtains close)

Act II Scene 3 Witches visit Prospero *(Half Set)*

(The Witches and Ariel enter through the auditorium)

Witch 1 We've been a wee while getting here. Did you take us by the scenic route?

Ariel We went 'Under the blossom that hangs on the bough.' The island is famous for it.

Witch 2 We could have flown here quicker.

Ariel And missed seeing the blossom?

Witch 3 And missed you lying in the cowslip's bells with the owls crying, and the bees sucking.

Witch 1 I think we could well have left out the sucking bees. Anything else to see before we get where we're going?

Ariel I was going to show you my flying bats.

Witch 2 What's special about flying bats? We have flying bats at home.

Witch 3 They're always in my hovel, getting in my hair…

Ariel I fly on their backs.

Witch 3 You fly on their backs? What size are your bats!?

Witch 1 Look, we're very grateful for your time, but we do need to see your master. Soon, if possible.

Ariel His cell is hidden in the cave above us.

Witch 2 *(Looking up)* That's a funny place for a cave.

Witch 3 I think he means up ahead. I see a crack opening.

(The curtains open on a Half Set – Prospero's Cell)

Witch 1 So this is how the owner of an island lives. I expected something on a bit of a grander scale.

Ariel Ah well, if the tourist trade had taken off – maybe…

(Prospero appears SR on stage)

Prospero Welcome to my humble home.

Witch 1 Well thank you. We got here – eventually.

Prospero I am sorry – my sprite is easily diverted. I am Prospero.

Witch 3 Aye – it says so in the book.

Prospero Does it indeed. Then you have the better of me.

Witch 2 We come from a coven near Cawdor. I'm Kirsty.

Witch 3 Bella.

Witch 1 And Morag.

Prospero Ladies, your names are unfamiliar to me – but may I assume you are associated with the party of voyagers who have just washed up on my shore.

Witch 1 Already? Your sprite said he was to send a Tempest to wreck them.

Prospero He was, he did, and they were. And I apologise for the inconvenience.

Witch 2 It's a little bit more than inconvenient. We had to guarantee their voyage.

Witch 3 There and back or their money back.

Prospero I had my reasons, which I now regret. But the good news is that all are safe and well.

Witch 1 And alive to make a claim on us.

Prospero That may be so, because the bad news is that they no longer have a boat.

Witch 2 They may be here for a wee while then.

Prospero Indeed. By the way, may I enquire as to how you three ladies arrived on the island.

Witch 3 Oh, we flew in.

Prospero Flew in? You talk as if this was a normal procedure.

Witch 2 Well, it was touch and go at times – a bit further than we're used to.

Ariel They fly on their besoms, master.

Prospero Really? Amazing! I've never heard of that before.

Witch 1 Broomsticks.

Prospero Oh, broomsticks. You have magic broomsticks?

Witch 1 You whip up storms, we whip around on broomsticks. It's a magic world we live in.

Prospero You might almost think we were works of fiction.

Witch 2 So, why did you order up a Tempest?

Witch 3 Which you now regret doing.

Prospero My daughter is young and innocent and, I have to say, good-looking – and I would not want the first man she meets to be a barbarian. So I secure the island with storms until the right man comes along.

Witch 1 Except that this crew survived, and so the first man she meets is either a Scottish murderer or a Danish pirate.

Witch 2 Or vice-versa.

Witch 3 Interesting choice.

Witch 1 Which did she choose?

Prospero I am glad to say that the women in the party were very protective of her.

Witch 2 Jealous more like. They'd keep her well away from their men.

Prospero You sound as if that comes from personal experience.

Witch 1 Aye, we've had our moments with them.

Prospero She has fallen in with one she calls Feely. Is that good?

Witch 3 She should be fine with Feely.

Witch 2 Feely has – learnt about life.

Witch 1 She will certainly teach her how to – handle men.

Prospero That's a relief. It had been a concern of mine, how she would handle men when she saw them.

Witch 1 Right – well, changing the subject quickly as I think we should, we need to discuss how we get our clients home.

Prospero You are right. Those who have seen the world would not want to remain here for the rest of their lives.

Witch 1 Exactly.

Prospero I will think about it.

Witch 1 If you would – only I don't think we can fly them all home on broomsticks.

(The curtains close)

Act II Scene 4 **Miranda's idea** *(Front of Tabs)*

(Enter SL Caliban carrying the deckchairs; Miranda SR)

Miranda You have a weight on your shoulders, Caliban.

Caliban I have three deck chairs on my shoulders, mistress Miranda.

Miranda Is this some sort of exercise? To keep you fit?

Caliban No, it's some sort of disagreement with the invaders.

Miranda Not invaders, Caliban. My father has allowed them come here.

Caliban You have your opinion, mistress, and I'll have mine.

Miranda Oh dear. What happened?

Caliban Not prepared to pay two ducats for a chair.

Miranda I see. That's the rate, is it?

Caliban High season, weekend afternoon…

Miranda We don't have a high season.

Caliban Says so on the tariff.

Miranda What tariff's that?

Caliban They disrespected me – called me Signor Jobsworth.

Miranda Caliban, I was hoping to ask for your help.

Caliban Always ready to help you, mistress.

Miranda But it involves working with the invaders, as you call them.

Caliban Working with them?

Miranda Yes.

Caliban After what they've done?

Miranda They are our guests, Caliban. My father says we should treat them well. With respect.

Caliban Respect!

Miranda We must provide entertainment.

Caliban Bashing the beach attendant seems to be their level!

Miranda I have been consulting my father's books.

Caliban Alright for those as can read.

Miranda There are volumes from all ages in his library – and a number appear to have come, by some magic, from the future.

Caliban My mother had magic.

Miranda Your mother had bad magic. That's why we're trapped on this island.

Caliban So you say – I don't remember. She's long gone now.

Miranda My father took on her magic, and made it good. He will get us away from the island.

Caliban Not me – this is my home. Me and the soap fairies – we'll stay here. Be a tourist attraction without the storms – good ticket.

Miranda So long as they pay for their deckchairs. Anyway, back to the entertainment. In one of the books, I found a game to play on the beach.

Caliban Not bashing the beach attendant.

Miranda Not bashing the beach attendant. In fact you may like to learn about it if you'll be having other tourists here. It could become popular.

Caliban What is it?

Miranda You have a net at head height and hit a ball over it.

Caliban Hit a ball over it?

Miranda That's right.

Caliban Mistress, there are many questions I could ask about this, but why would I want to hit a ball over a net?

Miranda So that the person on the other side can hit it back.

Caliban I see. And this is entertainment?

Miranda It will be, one day. Or so the book says.

Caliban I can't see it. What do you hit the ball with?

Miranda Your hands. But the entertainment is not just for the people playing – it is also for the people watching.

Caliban Watching people hitting a ball with their hands – over a net – on a beach.

Miranda Yes. And the clothes they wear to do it.

Caliban There's a uniform for this entertainment?

Miranda It's called a strip.

Caliban Is that like a beach attendant's uniform?

Miranda No, Caliban, it's nothing like a beach attendant's uniform. There's a lot less of it for a start.

(They exit SR)

Act II Scene 5 Beach Volleyball competition *(Full Set)*

(At the bar on the beach, as in Scene 2)

Macbeth Did ye think the barbecue last night was a success?

Hamlet Well – it was not entirely unpleasant.

Macbeth I couldn't quite place the meat we were offered on the spit. Some sort of bird was it?

Hamlet Feely did her best – with what the island could offer.

Macbeth Which was?

Hamlet It was not exactly a bird.

Macbeth What d'you mean, 'not exactly a bird'?

Hamlet Although it had wings and it flew.

Macbeth It's not a bird; it can't be a plane…

149

Hamlet And it is not Superman. But…

Macbeth But wha'?

Hamlet It is a bat, man. Or rather, it was.

Macbeth We've been eating bats?

Hamlet Not so loud. The others might hear.

(But Macbeth is already clearing his mouth)

Macbeth Yeugh!

(Beth closes in)

Beth I hope you're not poisoning my husband here.

Hamlet We do not poison the Scottish. We have enough to do poisoning our own people.

Beth I'm never sure about using poison. There's something more satisfying about the dagger. More hands-on, if you know what I mean.

Hamlet We are not unfamiliar with using steel ourselves. But poison will not attack back – unless of course you drink from the wrong cup.

Beth Ah yes, the Bard will have you do that. *(To Macbeth)* Are you alright now, man Mac? You're still alive.

Macbeth No thanks to last night's chef. The witches might have done better.

(Enter SL, on cue, the Witches with Prospero & Polonius)

Witch 1 The witches might have done better than what?

Macbeth Nothing – nothing at all. Not important. I spoke in jest.

Witch 2 Have ye no' learnt better than to jest about witches?

Witch 3 And jest when we were about to do you a favour, too.

Beth A favour from you? There's a novelty.

Prospero If I may interject? I have just been talking to these charming young ladies…

Glen He should've gone to Specsavers!

Prospero …these charming young ladies, and we have developed a plan.

Morangie Is the plan as well developed as the young ladies?

Witch 3 Is that a compliment, Kirsty?

Witch 2 Young ladies? – well!

Witch 1 Let's hope so for his sake.

Prospero It is a plan to get you all home. Off the isle.

Duncan Well, I'll be glad to hear it.

Glen Nice one, Dunc – off the isle; 'I'll be glad to hear it'!

Duncan It was no' a joke.

Morangie Dunc doesn't do jokes, Glen.

Glen Oh, sorry Dunc.

Macbeth And what is this plan?

Hamlet It will let us Danes off the hook if you can do it.

Beth Mmm – Danes on a hook – now there's an idea. Nice punishment for rape & pillage.

Macbeth Or for serving us bat on a spit.

Prospero If you will stop squabbling for a moment, I will tell you.

Witch 1 It's no good, they're always at it. Why don't we let them wait?

Witch 2 Aye – leave them in suspenders.

(Witches exit SL as Ophelia & Miranda enter SR)

Ophelia Did someone mention suspenders?

Hamlet Oh, trust you to come in on that cue, Feely!

Ophelia Come in with suspenders? Not my fault – it was in the script. What are you suggesting?

Miranda Ophelia has been teaching me many new things. Like how to deal with innuendo.

Ophelia You are lucky if you get innuendo with this lot – it is more often in your face! And do not say a word, Hammie – I did not mean that!

Hamlet Do not worry – I will keep my mouth shut, as usual!

Miranda But I still have much to learn.

Prospero *(To Polonius)* I am not sure if I am fully understanding this conversation, Polonius.

151

Polonius I am not sure that we should be, Prospero. I fear that daughters are a law unto themselves.

Ophelia Miranda has discovered a new type of entertainment.

Miranda And I would like you all to join in.

Prospero *(To Polonius)* This is the favour that I was mentioning earlier.

Polonius By the look of it, I think that it is finding favour with the men.

Prospero But they do not know what the entertainment is yet.

Polonius That does not appear to be a problem. Your daughter is holding their attention.

Prospero She is holding a book of rules.

Ophelia As Entertainments Officer on this cruise…

Duncan This grounded cruise.

Ophelia …I would like to invite Miranda to tell us more.

Glen Your dreams come true, Morangie?

Morangie One day they will invent an island like this and call it Ibiza.

Miranda We need two teams, a net and a ball.

(Enter SL Caliban and Ariel, with net and ball)

Caliban We have found a net and a ball.

Miranda So the teams will be the Scots against the Danes?

Beth It usually is.

Gertrude Quite like old times.

Miranda But you are not wearing appropriate strip.

Macbeth And what is the appropriate strip?

Miranda All will be revealed.

*(Ophelia and Miranda reveal they are wearing bikinis;
Exit SL Prospero & Polonius shaking their heads)*

Ophelia This is the appropriate strip, or so we're told.

Gertrude What sort of a game is this?

Beth I don't think it will catch on in the highlands, dressed like that.

Miranda All who play must wear the strip.

Duncan What, the men too?

Claudius That will just look silly.

Miranda Caliban and Ariel have costumes for you.

(The men are ushered SR to a place to change)

Gertrude I hope you are not expecting us senior ladies to expose ourselves in this way.

Beth Sadly, it may not be a pretty sight.

Miranda You can be the referees. They wear more clothes.

Gertrude But we do not know the rules.

Ophelia Nobody knows the rules – that makes it even.

Miranda We must clear a space for the game to be played.

(Caliban and Ariel reappear – business as they set up the net)

Beth *(Looking at the audience)* The beach seems to be a bit crowded.

Miranda They are the stuff of dreams. My father says so.

Beth You mean they're not really there.

Ophelia I think they will be wishing they are not really there soon.

(The men start drifting on dressed in swimming strip)

Gertrude Here are some other people who look as if they are wishing they were not here.

Macbeth Where's a man supposed to tuck his sporran wearing this?

Banquo I know I've only got a small part, but this is ridiculous

Birnam Me too.

Ophelia Hammie looks quite dishy in his.

Hamlet It is fine – one day all rowers will dress like this.

Miranda Where are the team captains?

Duncan That'll be me for the Scots.

Claudius And I for the Danes.

Miranda The book says you must toss for ends.

Ophelia I do not think they can both toss together, Miranda.

Duncan I wouldn't bet on it, lass.

Ophelia I think one of the referees must toss for them.

Beth I have a spare groat. Will that do?

Duncan Aye, we'll make do with that, Beth.

Beth Heads for Scots, tails for Danes. *(She tosses a coin)* Heads, Scots.

Claudius It is unfair. We did not see the coin.

Beth *(Showing him the coin)* Heads – see?

Duncan *(To Claudius)* It's only a friendly, man. We can have a proper scrap later if you're not happy with the result.

Ophelia Take your ends, and we will get on with the game.

Miranda Two people play from each team at a time. Change one person after a point is scored. First to 21 points.

Gertrude Is that really what it says in the book?

Ophelia No, I think these are local rules – but who cares?

Beth Who cares? Aye. I think I've heard that before. But it was by a blue bothy on a blasted heath.

Gertrude Are you away with the fairies again, Mrs Mac?

Beth Not the fairies. But I'm beginning to wonder what those witches are up to.

Gertrude Let us play the game and worry about witches later.

(The match begins – players swapping as needed. Add live commentary as required. At the end of the match, the winners are declared by the referees, Beth & Gertrude)

Act II Scene 6 Round-up *(Front of Tabs)*

(As the tabs close, Beth & Gertrude come forward)

Beth So you offered us a cruise to an exotic island, and this is it.

Gertrude Ya. It is an island, and it is exotic.

Beth Aye. If you call beach volleyball exotic.

Gertrude It was a new experience.

Beth True, but not one I'd want to experience every day.

Gertrude And Mr Prospero has turned into a good host.

Beth Aye, after wrecking us.

Gertrude And you cannot complain of the weather.

Beth No, but it's strange how quickly you can begin to long for the highland mists.

Gertrude I also think of Elsinore – but then I remember that the stones are cold and damp for most of the year.

Beth I miss the neighbours.

Gertrude Are you not always trying to kill one another?

Beth Aye. But I've heard it's not much better in the State of Denmark.

Gertrude Rotten.

Beth So, Prospero has a plan to get us home.

Gertrude I am told he is working on it.

Beth Let's hope he organises a smoother landing this time.

(They exit SL)

Act II Scene 7 **Heading for home** *(Full Set)*

(The Scottish men are back in the bar on the beach)

Duncan So, how are we getting home, Mac?

Macbeth What makes you think it's down to me?

Duncan Your wife got us into this, as I recall.

Macbeth And paid good money for a return trip. Speak to the organisers if you've a complaint.

Glen The organisers have made themselves scarce.

Morangie About as scarce as the whisky's getting now.

Duncan Aye, that's the really bad news. We may have to start drinking the Danes' lager.

Glen They seem to have an inexhaustible supply.

Morangie Makes you wonder where it's coming from.

Banquo It gives a whole new meaning to 'a wee dram'!

Birnam Don't even go there!

Macbeth Here comes the chief lager drinker now.

(Enter SR Hamlet with Claudius, Horatio, Yorick, Carl & Berg)

Hamlet Here are the Scottish, always at the bar.

Duncan When there's something worth drinking.

Macbeth We're thinking of forming an escape committee.

Carl We offer free lager, and you wish to escape?

Berg Incomprehensible!

Horatio This could be heaven on earth.

Hamlet There are more things in heaven & earth, Horatio, than are dreamt
of in your philosophy.

Yorick But not in the Scots' philosophy.

Hamlet Alas, poor Yorick, they do not see it.

Macbeth What are you Danes hammering on about?

Duncan It's the lager getting to them.

(Enter SR the ladies: Beth, Gertrude, Ophelia & Miranda)

Beth Don't you boys ever think of anything but where your next drink is
coming from?

Gertrude I suppose there are worse things for men to think about.

Beth True, but it gets monotonous.

Macbeth We were talking of getting home.

Duncan Aye, things are too quiet around here.

Gertrude It is good that the Danes and the Scots live here together in
harmony for a while.

Macbeth Wha' d'you mean? The Bard never had us fighting the Danes.

Duncan No, it was always good honest Scot on Scot.

Gertrude I do not know about the good and the honest, but you are right –
we Danes were involved in our own mischief. Usually behind an arras.

Beth It sounds like we're all getting homesick.

Miranda You all have homes to go to – I have only here.

Gertrude But here is paradise – if you know nothing else.

Ophelia But we have opened her eyes. Now she wants to see the world.

Macbeth And I think the world would very much like to see her! *(Beth goes for her dirk)* I mean the *rest* of the world.

Gertrude Well she may get her opportunity.

Hamlet She would have to get off this island first.

Gertrude We have been hearing rumours.

Beth Miranda was talking just now to that little Ariel chappie. What was it he said?

Miranda My father is planning to give him his freedom.

Macbeth Wha' does that mean to us?

Gertrude I think we shall soon find out. Have you noticed the witches have been away for a while?

Duncan And they can stay away for a good long while as far as I'm concerned.

Macbeth They got us into this fix in the first place.

Gertrude But maybe they will make amends.

Duncan Maybe your Danish bacon will fly!

Ophelia Let us see – they are coming now.

> *(Enter SL Witches with Prospero, Polonius, Caliban & Ariel*
> *– Prospero wears a 'Dr Who' long scarf & hat)*

Witch 3 We've been away, but now we're back.

Witch 2 With news for Hammie and for Mac.

Witch 1 Have you missed us?

Hamlet Well, we were just saying…

Macbeth We've missed you like a dose of the pox.

Witch 1 Oh, charming I'm sure.

Witch 2 Perhaps Mr Grumpy doesn't want to be part of our plot.

Witch 3 Perhaps he wants to stay here forever.

Beth Ignore Mr Grumpy. He'll get over it. What's the plot?

Witch 1 Well, for those who want to participate…

Witch 2 We've worked out a new travel deal.

Duncan Oh no, not another one!

Witch 3 This one's watertight.

Glen Unlike the Danes' boat.

Hamlet It was not the boat – it was the Tempest. We rowed into the wrong play.

Morangie And what form of travel would this new deal be?

Witch 1 A very advanced sort of transport.

Witch 2 Transport of the future.

Witch 3 You could say transport <u>to</u> the future.

Witch 2 Or the past.

Witch 1 Or anywhere you choose – or so we're told.

Gertrude Told by whom?

Witch 2 Good grammar Gertrude.

Witch 3 He is the object of the sentence.

Witch 1 True. But let's just say, the Doctor.

Macbeth Oh dear – I have visions of that blasted heath again.

Duncan And the blue bothy with the flashing light.

(We hear the sound of a Tardis landing)

Macbeth Tell me it's not the blue bothy with the flashing light.

(The Tardis arrives SL)

Beth It is the blue bothy with the flashing light.

Gertrude You have met it before?

Beth Not personally. But we have suffered the consequences…

Macbeth It brought us the football. Years ago.

Hamlet It stopped the rape & pillage.

(Prospero steps forward)

Prospero That is surely not such a bad thing.

Claudius It went well with the medieval times we lived in.

Beth *(Looking at the Tardis door)* Who is in there?

Prospero No – he is not.

Beth I beg your pardon?

Prospero The occupant is not in there.

Polonius Well that is not strictly true, Prospero. If he is not in there, he is not the occupant.

Prospero You are a pedant after my own heart, Polonius.

Polonius However, we have negotiated with the – erstwhile – occupant a means of escape.

Prospero If you enter here, you will be transported back to your rightful time and place.

Polonius Assuming that is what you want.

Banquo Well, since the whisky's run out…

Birnam And the only alternative here is gnat's water…

Duncan I think we're all for it. What do the rest of you say?

(General shouts of approval from the Scots)

Claudius And I think we Danes will also be happy to get home.

(General shouts of approval from the Danes)

Duncan Even without your boat.

Claudius We have many more longships at home.

Horatio Will we all fit in there?

Yorick It looks no bigger than a castle closet.

Witch 1 You'll be surprised when you get inside.

Witch 2 It opens up.

Witch 3 Just like a Tardis.

All *(except for Witches)* A what?

Witch 1 Never mind – in you get.

Witch 2 Inside for the ride.

> *(They all start to get in except for Ophelia, Miranda, Polonius,*
> *Prospero, Caliban, Ariel & Witches)*

Miranda But I have no time and place to go back to.

Polonius For you, Miranda, there is a special role. Is that not the case,
Prospero.

Prospero Indeed, daughter. The – erstwhile – occupant has told us that he
requires a new companion on his travels.

Polonius Through time and space.

Miranda Companion. And you, father. What will you do?

Prospero I shall be with you.

Miranda And the – erstwhile – occupant?

Prospero *(Hesitates)* He will be with us too.

Miranda *(Suspicious)* He will?

Polonius Come, let us get in.

Miranda And Caliban and Ariel?

Caliban I have an island to run, mistress.

Ariel With the help of us sprites, of course.

Caliban Tell your friends to visit us.

Ariel Guaranteed no Tempests.

> *(Polonius, Prospero, Ophelia and Miranda enter the Tardis,*
> *which then takes off with its usual sound)*

Ariel *(To the witches)* You are still here?

Witch 1 Och aye – we'll fly back the way we came.

Ariel Shall I find you three bats to fly on?

Witch 1 No, don't trouble yourself – we'll just dust off the broomsticks
again.

Witch 2 Apply the cream.

Witch 3 And take to the skies. *(Pause)* Anyway, didn't we eat all the bats?

Witch 1 Sssh! I think we'd better be on our way. Brooms this way. *(As they exit USL)* Byeee!

Caliban Well, what d'you make of that, master Ariel? Now we have the island all to ourselves. All to ourselves, and the …

Ariel … and the bats. Yes. Except that *(looks at the remains of the barbecue and holds up something on a skewer)* – something tells me we had better go and check up on those bats!

(The curtain falls)

*** END OF MACHAMLET GOES WEST ***

The musical bottles in MacHamlet

Director's Notes

These plays were designed to be performed as an entertainment at a medieval banquet. As such they do not require complex scenery or lighting, any more than Shakespeare himself did.

In production, we inserted an extra interval in Act I to enable the first course to be served, with a second course served during the 'official' interval between Acts I and II.

Put in local variations as you wish, and if you think you can improve on the quotes then do that too! Good luck with your show, and please have fun.

MacHamlet

The musical bottles in Act II Scene 2 were achieved by part-filling with liquid to obtain a scale. You will note that there are seven Danes and we found (surprisingly) that small Carlsberg bottles could be tuned to give seven notes of the tonic sol-fa scale. Each bottle was numbered, and the cast rearranged themselves in line so that they got it wrong twice, then correct the third time. With the Scotch whisky bottles on the bar, we found that a range of empty bottles of various brands gave us most of our scale (we needed to part-fill just one of them) – and we used a wine glass for our top note.

As a historical fact, Lady Godiva was a contemporary of Macbeth, though I'm not suggesting they ever met in real life – and certainly not at a football.

The 'football' match in Act II Sc 5 became more of a handball match due to constraints of the number of tables, chairs and diners in the auditorium. But frankly, by that time nobody cared!

And if you need help in constructing a Lego trophy, ask your children!!

Bard Again!

We gave each table a bag of Lego bricks during the interval asking them to construct a suitable trophy to replace the one broken by Macbeth earlier. Results were collected by the Witches in Act II Scene 6.

Bard Again! & MacHamlet Goes West

The 'football' match became Water Polo and Beach Volleyball respectively, but the chaos and mayhem remained the same!

PS I'm very happy for you to video your production – in fact I would recommend it. We have found that to show an early dress rehearsal to cast and crew in place of a straight rehearsal can be time well spent.

Pantomimes & Plays by John Owen Smith

Full length pantomimes (2 acts) with one interval:

- **Aladdin** The pantomime with the flying palace – 15 speaking parts + chorus
- **Ali Baba** Scheherazade introduces her very last Arabian Night's tale – 18 speaking parts + chorus
- **Cinderella** Baron Hardup's household as tradition tells it – with immortal lines – 14 speaking parts + chorus
- **Dick Whittington** and his cat – the tale as recorded by Fred Chaucer – 16 speaking parts + chorus
- **Humpty Dumpty** The Muffet Mob's on the loose – can old egghead save the day? – 16 speaking parts + 7 children speaking + chorus
- **Jack and the Beanstalk** Witch Whey's wicked wheeze won't work – will it? – 17 speaking parts + chorus
- **Nutcracker** The script Tchaikovsky might have set to music, if he'd known – 15 speaking parts + chorus
- **Puss in Boots** That talking cat gets everywhere – and gets his just desserts! – 15 speaking parts + chorus
- **Little Red Riding Hood** There could be a fete worse than death – ask the Wolf! – 16 speaking parts + chorus
- **Robin Hood** A cricket match in Sherwood Forest? There's Nun Better to play – 15 speaking parts + chorus
- **Sleeping Beauty** The show with an interval of a hundred years! – 11 speaking parts + chorus
- **Snow White and the 7 Dwarfs** The mirror's off the wall in more ways than one! – 18 speaking parts + chorus

Mini Pantomimes (in verse): **approx 15-20 mins run time**

- **Cinderelder** Prince Charming gets a bit fed up with Cinderella after 20 years! – 9 speaking parts
- **Bleeding Moody** Can you imagine the Sleeping Beauty as a teenager of today? – 6 speaking parts

Full length plays (2 acts) with one interval:

- **Flora's Heatherley** An historical play based on Flora Thompson's time in Grayshott 1898–1901 – 20 speaking parts
- **Flora's Peverel** An historical play based on Flora Thompson's time in Liphook 1916–1928 – 25 speaking parts
- **The Broomsquire** Adapted from the novel by Sabine Baring-Gould – 20 speaking parts (can be performed by 10 people)

www.ingramcontent.com/pod-product-compliance
Lightning Source LLC
Chambersburg PA
CBHW060252050426
42448CB00009B/1625